The Demise of Diversity?

A COMPARATIVE PROFILE OF EIGHT TYPES OF INSTITUTIONS

by C. Robert Pace

Professor of Education
University of California, Los Angeles

A Technical Report Sponsored by
The Carnegie Commission on Higher Education

*The Carnegie Commission on Higher Education,
2150 Shattuck Avenue, Berkeley, California 94704,
has sponsored the preparation of this report as
part of a continuing effort to obtain and present
significant information for public discussion. The
views expressed are those of the author.*

THE DEMISE OF DIVERSITY?
A Comparative Profile of Eight Types of Institutions

Library of Congress catalog card number 74-75158.

Contents

Foreword

As part of our efforts to provide a comprehensive survey of higher education in the United States, the Carnegie Commission on Higher Education sponsored a series of profiles of several significant types of institutions within our higher educational system. These profiles study such institutions as the Catholic and Protestant colleges, private colleges, state colleges, and multicampus universities. C. Robert Pace, who contributed to this series with his study of Protestant colleges, now looks at the entire network of higher education. With the results of questionnaires administered to both alumni and upperclassmen, he is able to classify institutions into eight distinct sectors, to analyze how each sector differs from the others in its character, environment, and student clientele, and to determine in what ways these differences may be diminishing. The "profile of profiles" that Professor Pace has developed thus provides a clear, schematic overview of important aspects of our educational system.

Clark Kerr

Chairman
Carnegie Commission
on Higher Education

February 1974

Acknowledgments

A questionnaire survey of students and alumni from a diverse set of colleges and universities across the country forms the data base for this report. The survey was a major activity of the higher education evaluation program in the Center for the Study of Evaluation, Graduate School of Education, UCLA. The center is a federally supported research and development organization in the field of education. It is now funded through the National Institute of Education, but during the period in which this survey was carried out its funding came from the U.S. Office of Education. Dr. Marvin Alkin is the director of the center and Dr. Richard Seligman is the associate director. I am indebted to both of them for professional and administrative assistance, and to the U.S. Office of Education for its financial support. There is no longer a special higher education program within the center. Instead, a new organization, the Higher Education Laboratory, which is an interdisciplinary center for research, evaluation, policy studies, and information in the field of higher education, has been created at UCLA.

Over the period of several years when this survey was being planned, carried out, and preliminary analyses of results were made, many graduate student research assistants, administrative and clerical personnel, and professional colleagues contributed to it—and to all of them my thanks and appreciation.

For this particular report I have drawn upon the computer expertise of Dr. Ricardo Klorman, who produced the various comparisons between types of institutions, the factor analyses, z scores, and the like. In assembling and writing this report—preparing charts and graphs and tables, looking up data from prior analyses, getting the manuscript in shape, and handling all administrative matters—I am especially indebted to my administrative and research assistant, Barbara McCaslin.

C. Robert Pace

1. Profiles of Diversity

Conflicting pressures toward conformity and diversity are not new in education or in other aspects of American life. The automobile industry, for example, began with diversity, moved toward conformity, and is now moving again toward diversity. Higher education began with conformity, moved toward diversity, and perhaps now is moving again toward greater conformity.

From the early days of the auto industry one recalls such names as Reo, Hupmobile, Franklin, Packard, Nash, Essex, Pierce-Arrow, Stutz, and many others, none of which are produced today. Subsequently, most of the industry was consolidated into the three major corporations of General Motors, Ford, and Chrysler. For a period of several decades the products of the "big three" monopolized the American highways and reflected a common trend toward bigger, heavier, and more powerful machines. Within the past decade, diversity has re-emerged, mainly through the import market for such well-known and popular products as Toyota, Datsun, and Mazda from Japan; Volkswagen, Porsche, BMW, and Mercedes from Germany; MG, Triumph, Austin and others from England; Italy's Fiat, Sweden's Volvo, and France's Renault and Peugeot. This in turn stimulated the "big three" to extend the range of their own products mainly by introducing smaller and more compact models.

In the early history of higher education the colonial colleges, despite their sectarian differences, were essentially molded in the British tradition of what today we would call the liberal arts. Dotting the landscape as the population moved westward in the 19th century are hundreds of liberal arts colleges—in Pennsylvania, Ohio, Indiana, Illinois, and other states to the North and South and far West. Most of them, like the early colonial colleges, were founded by Protestant denominations, and many are still affiliated with the church. They were often the frontier counterparts of the earlier colonial colleges, centers of education and evangelism in a harsh environment. The Ivy League universities in the East, which grew from this same heritage, are today nonsectarian although most of them remain private institutions rather than creatures of the state.

As the 19th century passed its midpoint, the movement for the establishment of public higher education gained momentum. Most of the major state universities today, from Ohio to California, were established in the last half of the 19th century, owing much to the impetus of the Land-Grant Act of Congress in 1862 and to the industrialization of a nation that wanted specialists and better practitioners in agriculture, engineering and mechanical arts, mining, forestry, and other technical fields as much or more than clergymen or cultured gentlemen. The history of higher education also includes the establishment of women's colleges, theological seminaries, vocational and technical institutes, teachers colleges, Catholic schools, military schools and, most recently, the junior colleges.

One result of this varied heritage has been, at least to some extent, a kind of selective mating between students and colleges. Many Catholic youth have gone to Catholic colleges. Many Methodist youth have gone to Methodist colleges. The old normal schools and teachers colleges provided training for large numbers of young women interested in becoming schoolteachers. The growth of higher education did not come by providing the same kinds of programs for larger numbers of students. Rather, by introducing new programs higher education became relevant and attractive to larger numbers of students. Programs in engineering, agriculture, business, home economics and other fields brought to the campuses students who would not have gone at all if the course of study had been limited to moral philosophy, mathematics, literature, and Latin.

For roughly one hundred years, from the mid-nineteenth to the mid-twentieth centuries, the growth of higher education was marked by increased diversity of institutions and of clientele. While diversity is still a word commonly used in describing higher education, evidence accumulated during the past two decades suggests a new trend toward greater homogeneity. In his book for the Carnegie Commission, *Institutions in Transition: A Profile of Change in Higher Education,* Harold Hodgkinson documents what appears to be a drift toward a greater conformity. Some two-year colleges have become four-year colleges. Many four-year colleges offering only an undergraduate degree now also offer a master's degree. Most teachers colleges have become state colleges. Many state colleges have become state universities. In each case the effect of change has been to blur the distinctions between the various types of institutions. As each institution expands the range of its own programs, it may increase the diversity of its own clientele but at the same time decrease the difference between it and other institutions.

The dramatic growth in the past 20 years has been the expansion of publicly supported higher education. In 1950, for the first time in American higher education, the number of students enrolled in publicly supported institutions was equal to the number enrolled in privately supported institutions. Today the enrollment ratio between public and private is roughly three to one. Insofar as the large publicly supported institutions share many common characteristics, the room for diversity within the total system of higher education has thereby shrunk. Moreover, as the source of support has fallen more heavily upon state taxpayers and upon the research and training priorities of the federal government, the opportunities for institutions to be different have probably also been reduced.

Diversity among institutions of higher education, like competition in business and industry, is assumed to be desirable. It provides motivation for distinctiveness and efficiency and it enlarges the choices available to consumers. Just as trends toward monopoly in business are viewed as bad for the economy, and are therefore resisted by legislation and trust-busting activities, so also trends toward monopoly in higher education may be viewed as bad for the spirit. In education, however, there are no comparable mechanisms for holding such trends in check.

The virtue of variety and of the provision of multiple options for students has been an important theme in many of the publications sponsored by the Carnegie Commission on Higher Education. Thirteen of the volumes sponsored by the Commission are described as a series of profiles. Seven of these profiles analyze the characteristics of presumably distinctive types of institutions—Catholic colleges, state colleges and regional universities, two-year colleges, Negro colleges, private liberal arts colleges, small private colleges with limited resources, and Protestant colleges. Five of the profiles focus on programs and emphases that have come into prominence in the development of higher education and that in many respects cut across different types of institutions—for example, international programs, research institutes, professional education, science, and the arts. The other profile was the one previously noted which documented some tendency for institutions to become more like one another. Although it is primarily a study of academic governance, the Commission-sponsored volume entitled *The Multicampus University* can also be viewed as a profile of some of the large complex universities, particularly in those states where a statewide system of public universities has developed. These profiles taken together form an invaluable source for understanding different segments of higher education both currently and historically.

In his profile of Catholic higher education, Andrew Greeley identifies 350 Catholic colleges and universities. He notes that there is substantial diversity among these institutions—from very small Catholic girls schools operated primarily by members of the sponsoring order to major universities such as Notre Dame, where a substantial portion of the faculty are laymen, including many non-Catholics. The title of his profile, *From Backwater to Mainstream,* reflects the direction of change that has been occurring. Students in Catholic colleges and Catholic students in non-Catholic colleges are not much different from other students, not only in respect to their career aspirations but also in many of their social attitudes and values and intellectual interests. While the Catholic campus generally retains a warm and friendly atmosphere and a pervasive concern with Catholic values, the parochial insulation that characterized many Catholic institutions in an earlier day has in more recent times been rapidly disappearing.

In their profile of small private colleges with limited resources, *The Invisible Colleges,* Alexander Astin and Calvin Lee put nearly 500 colleges into that category. They are identified mainly by their small size (more than 70 percent of them have fewer than 1000 students) and by their lack of affluence both financially and in the selectivity of the student body. One-fourth of these institutions are Catholic, a third are nonsectarian, and the rest are Protestant. In contrast with large institutions, and in common with other small colleges, they provide a warm and more cohesive environment and more opportunities for students to participate in campus activities. While the so-called invisible colleges comprise about 18 percent of all the institutions, they account for only 5 percent of the total enrollment in higher education.

Morris Keeton's profile of private liberal arts colleges, *Models and Mavericks,* lists in the appendix 700 such institutions. These include independent colleges, Catholic colleges, and Protestant colleges. Among the independent colleges are ones that have achieved national prominence for their academic excellence and distinction and whose programs have been influential models for other institutions. Many of these model and maverick institutions provide a superior environment for the personal, social, and intellectual development of their students.

The profile of Protestant colleges, *Education and Evangelism,* by the present writer, noted that colleges affiliated with the mainline Protestant denominations were generally similar to other liberal arts colleges but that institutions related to the more evangelical and fundamentalist sects were in many respects distinctive in their environment and in the attainments and educational benefits claimed by their students and alumni.

Each of these profiles overlaps in some respects one or more of the other profiles. Astin and Lee include Catholic, Protestant and nonsectarian institutions. Keeton includes Protestant as well as independent colleges and also some evangelical colleges. The profile of Protestant colleges includes some which are now legally independent from their initial Protestant heritage. With the exception of some of the large Catholic institutions, each of the profiles, however, deals mainly with relatively small liberal arts colleges.

Alden Dunham's profile of state colleges and regional universities covers a different sector of higher education. These are publicly supported institutions. The author indicates that there were 279 such institutions in 1967 and that they accounted for 20 percent of the total enrollment in higher education. Many of them were initially teachers colleges, changing their names to state colleges and in some cases to state universities as new programs and new curricula were added. Teacher training nevertheless remains an important part of their program. The American Council on Education's annual survey of entering freshmen in 1968 showed that 42 percent of the students enrolling in state colleges planned to enter teaching as their vocational field. Dunham expresses concern that some of these institutions may have been changing from superior teachers colleges into mediocre universities. The drive toward obtaining university status is strong in some cases, however, and is nicely epitomized by a quote from Dunham's book, "someday we'll play in the Rose Bowl."

The profiles of Negro institutions and of two-year colleges, while important in their own right, are not discussed further here because the types of institutions that are described and compared in the present volume are limited to four-year institutions, and because the data collected in the present study are not sufficient for treating the predominantly Negro institutions as a special type.

The other profiles in the Carnegie series, as noted previously, do not focus on particular types of institutions but rather deal with special emphases and programs such as science, the arts, and professional and vocational emphases. These program emphases are reflected in varying degrees in the different types of institutions that are analyzed and compared in the present volume.

One of the interesting and valuable features of the various profiles that have been published is that each profiler has approached his topic in his own individual way. Some of them have drawn heavily on statistical surveys and census data. Others have included historical analyses. Still others have drawn upon the annual surveys of entering freshmen conducted by the research division of the American Council on Education. Still other profiles have drawn upon data collected by the National Opinion Research Center, including surveys of students and of alumni, and a special study of Catholic education. In most of the profiles, impressions gained from visits to selected campuses are also reported.

When UCLA's Center for the Study of Evaluation was established in the summer of 1966, one of its programmatic activities was the design and conduct of a comparative evaluation of different types of colleges and universities, based primarily on questionnaire responses from students and alumni. The results of this comparative evaluation form the substance of the present volume. The design and data base of the study are described in the next chapter. The basis for classifying institutions into various types is described at this point. The typology overlaps in many ways with some of the profiles in the Carnegie Commission series, and to this extent the present report provides a comparative integration of some of these profiles.

Eight types of institutions whose historical development, programs, and clientele have given them a distinctive character or personality are herewith noted.

Liberal arts colleges

Nearly all liberal arts colleges are privately supported rather than public or state-supported institutions. Most are relatively small—from 300 to 3000 students; most are located in relatively small towns and cities rather than in the midst of urban complexes; and most are residential. The students who attend these colleges describe the atmosphere as friendly and congenial. The students know one another. The professors are friendly, and know the students. Beyond this sense of community, which is characteristic of nearly all liberal arts colleges, there are distinctive characteristics of some colleges. Some, for example, are distinguished for their intellectual strength. The students are selected from among the top high school graduates; the academic demands are rigorous; many students go to graduate or professional school after completing their BA degree in a program that combines a broad liberal education with specialization in an academic discipline. Others are distinguished by their religious and spiritual strength. Many small Catholic schools and schools connected with the more evangelical Protestant churches have a clearly religious atmosphere and emphasis.

In our subsequent analyses we will refer to three types of liberal arts colleges as follows:

SLA = highly selective liberal arts colleges, private, nonsectarian, strongly intellectual

DLA = strongly denominational liberal arts colleges. Catholic or evangelical Protestant

GLA = general liberal arts colleges, some denominational and some nonsectarian, but not as strongly denominational as DLAs nor as highly selective or intellectual as SLAs.

Universities

The large comprehensive university—having a variety of undergraduate programs and offering master's, doctor's and advanced professional degrees—is best exemplified by most state universities and by large private institutions such as Southern California, Syracuse, or New York University. Today some of them enroll 40,000 students, as at Michigan State and Minnesota. They are complex, heterogeneous institutions—like big cities compared with small towns.

Within this broad category, there are two subcategories that can be distinguished. As in the case of liberal arts colleges, one of these distinctions is based on selectivity and scholarship. Yale, Harvard, the other Ivy League universities, other private universities such as Duke, Chicago, and Stanford, plus some state universities having rather high admissions standards and scholastic demands such as the University of Michigan and the various campuses of the University of California are examples of institutions of this type. The other subcategory consists of institutions that are typically larger in size and scope than liberal arts colleges but not as comprehensive in graduate and professional school offerings as the major state universities. They do not usually, for example, offer advanced degrees in such professional fields as law or medicine, nor do they offer Ph.D.-level graduate work in a broad range of academic disciplines. Most commonly, these institutions are called state colleges or regional universities. The California state universities and colleges are examples, and often the regional nature of the institution is suggested by the title, as Western Michigan compared with Michigan State University. Although nearly all schools in this group are public, there are some private institutions that are also included.

In presenting the results of our survey we will refer to three types of universities as follows:

SU = highly selective and comprehensive universities, some public but mostly private, nonsectarian

SCOU = state colleges and other less comprehensive universities

GU = general comprehensive universities, mostly public but some private

Others

Finally, to round out our typology we identify institutions that have a primary occupation or subject-matter focus. An obvious example is teachers colleges. Today, few colleges that in fact have a predominant emphasis on teacher training are still called teachers colleges, most now being state colleges with a somewhat broader range of offerings. But there are colleges in which the training of teachers and other personnel for the public schools constitutes the major portion of the program. The other example consists of colleges and universities that have a predominant emphasis on engineering and the sciences. So, our last two categories are designated as follows:

TC   = colleges having a major emphasis on teacher training

ES   = colleges and universities having a major emphasis on engineering and science

The basis for defining these eight types of college environments comes primarily from a questionnaire called College and University Environment Scales. Commonly referred to as CUES, this instrument consists of statements about facilities, rules, customs, courses, faculty, events, student interests and activities and other conditions that may, or may not, be generally true or characteristic of a particular campus. It is a device for measuring the collective perception, the commonly shared beliefs, about the environment held by those who live in and are part of the environment. Students who are familiar with the college from having attended it for more than a year (usually upperclassmen) serve as reporters, indicating whether in their experience and perception the condition or event described by each of the statements is true about their college. When there is a division of opinion among the reporters about a particular statement, it is not counted in the score. But when there is consensus among the reporters by a margin of two to one or greater, the statement is regarded as being characteristic of the campus. The score for the college is based on the number of statements reaching this level of consensus.

There are five scores obtained from the test, each based on a set of 20 statements that define a broad characteristic or attribute of the environment. These scales, with examples of statements from them, are as follows:

1. Scholarship   An environment characterized by intellectuality and scholastic discipline, intellectual achievement, and the pursuit of knowledge. For example: "Students set high standards of achievement for themselves." "Most courses require intensive study and preparation out of class."

2. Awareness   An environment that encourages concern about social and political problems, individuality and expressiveness through the arts, and tolerance of criticism. For example: "Students are actively concerned about national and international affairs." "The school offers many opportunities for students to understand and criticize important works in art, music, and drama."

3. Community A friendly, cohesive, group-oriented campus. For example: "The school has a reputation for being friendly." "The professors go out of their way to help you."

4. Propriety An atmosphere that is mannerly, considerate, proper, and conventional. For example: "Students are conscientious about taking good care of school property." "Students are expected to report any violation of rules and regulations."

5. Practicality An environment characterized by enterprise, organization, material benefits, social activities, vocational emphasis, and orderly supervision. For example: "Frequent tests are given in most courses." "There is a recognized group of student leaders on campus." "It's important socially here to be in the right club or group."

An institution's score on each of these five dimensions constitutes a profile of its environment. Computer programs to identify profile similarities or clusters were applied to the scores of some 235 colleges and universities, with the computer printing out the names of institutions falling into each of the various clusters that emerged. Consistently, one of the clusters included almost exclusively the strongly denominational colleges, another consisted of highly selective nonsectarian liberal arts colleges, and still another consisted of colleges and universities having a primary emphasis on engineering and the sciences. Other clusterings of profile similarities were not as sharply defined, but in each case the majority of institutions in the cluster were of a similar type, that is, SU, GU, SCOU, GLA, or TC. It was from these analyses that the definition of eight types of institutional environments was derived.

Subsequently, a new set of 100 institutions was invited to administer CUES to samples of their upperclassmen in 1965, thus providing a cross-validation of the typology and a comparative base for interpreting CUES scores. These results, with the scores converted to percentiles, are shown in Figure 1.

From the profiles one can clearly see that the selective universities (SU) and selective liberal arts colleges (SLA) are very high on the scholarship and awareness scales, and that this is true not only for the average institution within the type but for all institutions of that type (the length of the bars extends to include all institutions whose scores are reported). Similarly, one can see that the special purpose institutions (ES and TC) are also fairly homogeneous in that the differences

FIGURE 1 Differences in college environments: CUES profiles for different types of institutions

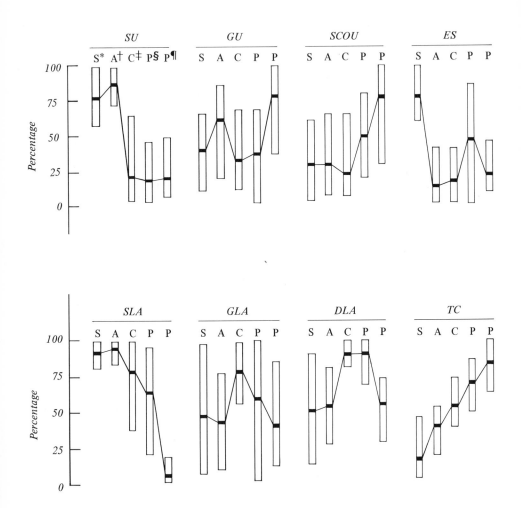

* Scholarship
† Awareness
‡ Community
§ Propriety
¶ Practicality

among institutions within the types are generally small (except on the propriety score for the ES schools). In contrast, the general liberal arts colleges (GLA) have scores that run the gamut from top to bottom, or nearly so, on all scales except community. On that scale all of them have higher than average scores. The strongly denominational colleges (DLA) have uniformly high scores on both community and propriety. There is a good deal of spread on all scales for the general comprehensive universities (GU) and the state colleges and other universities (SCOU). Both types tend to have high scores on practicality. On the awareness scale GUs tend to be higher than SCOUs but there is much overlap. Nearly all universities (SU, GU, and SCOU) rank below the 50th percentile on the community scale and nearly all liberal arts colleges (SLA, GLA, DLA) rank above the 50th percentile on that scale.

Clearly there are differences in the environments of these eight types of institutions. Any study of higher education on a national scale must take into account this diversity for the nature of one's college experience may depend to some extent on the sort of college one attends and this, in turn, may have a bearing on one's subsequent views and attainments.

To provide more recent data about the college environment, we included a short version of CUES, consisting of four items from each of the five scales, in the questionnaire we sent to upperclassmen in the spring of 1969 as part of the present study. The period from 1965 to 1969 was a period of student activism on many campuses, and therefore the environmental profiles may have changed from the ones shown in Figure 1. Comparisons of the rank order of the eight institutional types on each of the five CUES scales for 1965 *vs* 1969 resulted in the following rank order correlations: scholarship, .98; awareness, .73; community, .70; propriety, .58, and practicality, .80. On the scholarship scale no institutional type differed by more than one rank on the 1969 *vs* 1965 results. On the community scale no type differed on the two occasions by more than 2 ranks. On the propriety scale the relatively low correlation is owing to the fact that in 1969 there was no longer a very discriminating spread of scores on that scale, with all scores falling in the lower half of the potential range of scores. On the practicality scale, the only notable difference was an increase from a rank of 6 to a rank of 3.5 for the ES schools. Except for the propriety scale, which no longer appears to be very useful, these correlations indicate that the relative ranking of the eight types of institutions on other aspects of the college environment has not significantly changed.

There are two other characteristics of the college environment that we shall be considering as we analyze the results of our surveys: one is the size of the institution and the other is the academic selectivity of the student body. The definition of size is self-evident. The colleges from which our upperclassmen and alumni samples were drawn range from a few hundred students to more than 40,000. The definition of academic selectivity needs to be explained. Today the most widely used indicators are the scores of entering students on the College Entrance Examination Board's Scholastic Aptitude Test, or on the tests in the American College Testing Program, or the students' high school grades. Testing programs were not in operation on a really massive scale at the time our sample of alumni entered college. Nevertheless institutions were, and are, selective in many ways. Indeed, going to college at all was a fairly selective decision in the 1940s: about one out of nine young people of college age were in college in 1950, compared with about five out of nine today. Traditionally, going to college has been associated with having made good grades in a college preparatory course of study in high school and having grown up in a family environment where college attendance was more or less expected. Using these traditional indicators, we devised a scale from some of our questionnaire items to identify alumni, who at the time of college entrance, might have been described as "college prone." This index is as follows: (1) having made B+ grades or better in high school, (2) having attended a high school where all or most of the graduates went to college (implying a precollege emphasis in the high school curriculum), (3) having grown up in an environment with 100 or more books in the home, and (4) in a family where one or both parents had gone to college. With that sort of background, and assuming adequate financial means, a student would probably be eligible for admission to almost any college or university. In our population of alumni, 27 percent of the group had either three or all four of these precollege characteristics. Looking only at this group of "college-prone" individuals we can see how they are distributed among the different types of institutions in our study. We find, for example, that 51 percent of the student body at the highly selective liberal arts colleges (SLAs) were in this "academic prone" category, and by way of contrast, 13 percent of the student body at the predominantly teacher training colleges (TCs) were in the "academic prone" group. The proportions for each of the eight types of institutions are shown in Figure 2.

We did not derive a "college prone" index from our upperclassmen survey questionnaire, partly because the weight which it gives to family background seems less relevant today than was the case 20 years ago. Instead, we simply noted the percentage of students in each of the institutional types who reported that their high school grades were B+ or better. The rank order of our institutional types on this item of information correlates .85 with their rank order on Astin's Selectivity Index for the same institutions as reported in *Who Goes Where to College,* 1965. In Figure 3 we report the proportions of these B+ stu- —

dents, both for the upperclassmen and for the alumni samples. The college environment, then, can be characterized by the sort of people who are in it—in this case the proportion of academically oriented individuals in the student body. In this respect, as in others, there are clear differences between the various types of institutions.

Since the main purpose of this book is to examine some of the dimensions of diversity that characterize the system of higher education, we turn next to the design and content and data base of the surveys on which this examination rests.

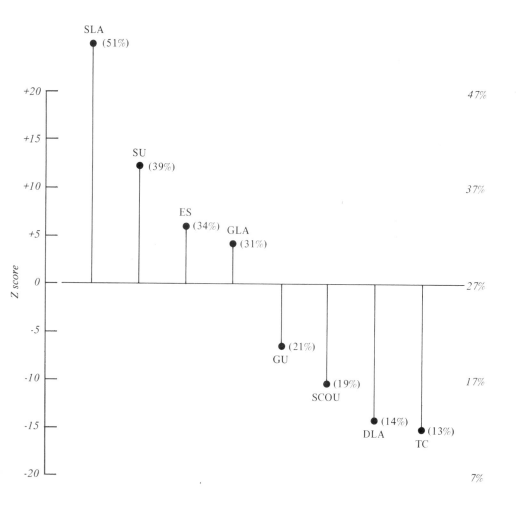

FIGURE 2   Academic selectivity: Percent of college-prone alumni in each type of institution

FIGURE 3a Academic selectivity: Percent of upperclassmen from each type of institution whose high school grades were B+ or better

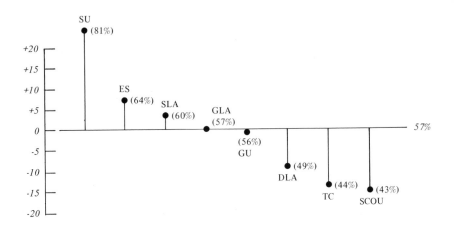

FIGURE 3b Academic selectivity: Percent of alumni from each type of institution whose high school grades were B+ or better

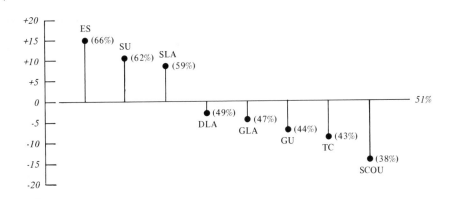

2. Design and Data

The data base for our comparisons of institutional types comes from two questionnaire surveys—one addressed to alumni and one addressed to upperclassmen. The alumni were from the graduating class of June 1950. The upperclassmen were end-of-year juniors who would be graduating in 1970. In both cases the questionnaires were distributed during the calendar year 1969.

Initially, we hoped to have 100 colleges participate in the survey—with an effort to get 10 institutions as representative of each of the eight types, except for the general liberal arts colleges (GLA), which were to be represented by 20, and the comprehensive universities (GU), which were also to be represented by 20—the GLAs because nationally there are more institutions of that type than of any other, and the GUs because there are more students in that type of environment than in any other. Our choice of institutions was based partly on the fact that each was regarded as a good example of its type—in much the same way that certain types of securities (rails, industrials, utilities, etc.) are selected to comprise the Dow-Jones index. The resulting composite is not a national *sample* of institutions or of students or alumni. Instead we refer to it as a national *baseline*. The institutions in our composite were deliberately selected from different parts of the country, and from the public and private sectors. Our planned sample of alumni included about equal numbers of individuals from public and private institutions—an accurate reflection of student enrollments as of 1950. The upperclassmen survey had a larger proportion of respondents from public institutions, a difference consistent with the national trend in enrollments but not, in the present case, as great a difference as the national trend would require in order to be fully representative.

Not all institutions invited to participate were able to do so, with the result that our alumni population came from 74 institutions and the upperclassmen population from 79. Sixty-seven institutions were common to both surveys.

For the alumni survey and from the larger institutions (those with undergraduate enrollments of 5,000 or more), we requested the names and current addresses of 300 graduates of the class of June 1950. The names were chosen at random, usually by picking every *n*th person from the graduation list. From the smaller institutions (those with undergraduate enrollments of less than 5,000), we requested a sample of 150. In a few small colleges, where the number of graduates was less than 150, additional names were picked from the classes of 1949 and 1951 so as to obtain a total sample of 150 names.

For the upperclassmen survey, the corresponding sample sizes were 200 from the larger institutions and 100 from the smaller ones. The upperclassmen questionnaires were administered by a local representative at the campus—sometimes by distributing them through the campus mail, sometimes by inviting students to come to a designated testing place, or in other ways suitable to local conditions. The selection of individuals was made locally, following recommended procedures intended to obtain a representative population.

During January and February 1969 we mailed questionnaires to the approximately 15,900 alumni whose names and addresses we had been given by the 74 participating colleges and universities. To stimulate a reasonably good response, we sent a post card reminder and, a month or two later, a second copy of the questionnaire to those who had not yet replied. We estimate that about 10 percent of the sample never received the questionnaire owing to incorrect addresses. From those who did receive it we had returns from 58 percent. The upperclassmen questionnaires were distributed in the spring of 1969, and from this population we had returns from 66 percent. The response rates need to be kept in mind, for obviously there were many alumni and upperclassmen who did not fill out their questionnaire. The best assumption to make is that those who did respond tended to be more favorably inclined toward their college and their own experiences; therefore the resulting picture one might draw of higher education would be a bit more positive or optimistic than would be revealed by a more complete set of responses. This likelihood does not seriously invalidate comparisons between the various types of institutions, however, because the direction of bias within each type is probably similar. Moreover, in this report we are not primarily making judgments about the experiences, attainments, or attitudes of students and alumni per se; rather our comments are centered on the comparative differences between the eight institutional types.

Further information about the data base is given in Table 1. The alumni sample of questionnaire respondents is more heavily weighted with men graduates than it should be, especially in the various university categories (SU, GU, SCOU). Two-thirds of the alumni group are males. This may be accounted for partly by the preponderance of males in colleges and universities in the years immediately following the end of World War II. It might also be influenced by the possibility that alumni offices find it easier to keep track of men graduates than they do women, owing to women's change of name with marriage. The main reason the sample includes a preponderance of men, however, is because we included in it the graduates of some eight colleges of engineering and science, nearly all of whom are men. The alumni data base also includes too many women in the selective liberal arts group (SLA), mainly because three of the institutions were women's colleges, with only one being a men's college. For the upperclassmen data base, the overall proportion of men and women is about right, but there are disproportional numbers in some of the institutional types—for example, too many women in GLA, SCOU, and TC. These differing proportions of men and women in the various institutional types could have a confounding influence on the interpretation of institutional differences. Because of this possibility we computed a number of correlations comparing the rank order of institutional types based solely on the responses of men *vs* the rank order based solely on the responses of women. For this purpose we selected various topics on which we thought there might be major sex differences—such as participation in activities related to science, religion, art, music, drama, literature, international and intercultural affairs; attitudes about government, the role of women, and civil rights; and estimated progress toward various personal and social and liberal education objectives. Of 26 such correlations (13 on the alumni data and 13 on the upperclassmen data), 4 were .90 or higher, 8 others were between .80 and .89, 9 were between .70 and .79, and 5 were below .70. Given these generally high correlations for the most extreme possible condition, it seems clear that the rank order of institutional types is affected very little by the proportion of men *vs* women respondents within the various institutional types.

Having described the population to which our surveys were addressed we turn now to describe the content of the questionnaires and, more broadly, the rationale of our inquiry. When the survey was being planned some years ago, several ideas and beliefs influenced the decisions about its content and purpose.

Growth in knowledge and understanding, intellectual skills and interests, heightened awareness, appreciation, values, attitudes, citizenship, moral sensitivity, and activities as producers and consumers of "the good life"—all these and more are commonly discussed among the objectives of higher education. Yet such a broad range of goals has seldom been dealt with in systematic evaluations of higher education. More frequently, judgments about the quality of institutions have been based on only one type of criterion—their assumed or measured intellectuality, such as student scores on a battery of standardized achieve-

TABLE 1   Data base for alumni and upperclassmen survey questionnaires

| Type of institution | Alumni survey population | | | | |
| | Number of respondents | | | Response rate | Number of institutions |
	Men	Women	Total		
Universities					
SU	519	224	743	55%	5
GU	1357	329	1686	56	12
SCOU	471	159	630	52	5
Liberal arts					
SLA	274	450	724	69	7
GLA	933	599	1532	60	17
DLA	462	352	814	54	10
Other					
ES	1060	23	1083	61	8
TC	575	467	1042	52	10
TOTAL	5651	2603	8254	58	74

ment tests or the proportion of students who go on to graduate school. Many colleges and universities which score necessarily low when measured by an intellectual yardstick because of the nature of the student body they serve, may be highly effective in other respects such as the amount of change produced in their students or the role of their graduates in community service and active citizenship. As the country approaches more or less universal higher education, evaluations based on a single criterion not only are increasingly inadequate but may lead to a distorted national perspective on the different roles and differential effectiveness of higher education's institutions.

Moreover, most evaluations have been concerned with individual differences as the unit of analysis rather than with institutional differences. Yet higher education in any organized sense takes place in some sort of institutional setting. As noted in Chapter 1, there are some clear distinctions among different types of institutional settings. With more than half of the nation's high school graduates now going to college and distributing themselves among institutions which in many cases differ radically from one another, it seems reasonable to suppose that the nature of the college experience itself as well as the subsequent progress and attainment of students are associated with the institutional context in which it occurs.

Thus two basic decisions were made: one, that the scope of objectives and attainments to be measured should reflect a diversity of individual

Upperclassmen survey population				
Number of respondents			Response rate	Number of institutions
Men	Women	Total		
220	166	386	55%	4
866	612	1478	57	13
520	647	1167	76	10
367	290	657	79	8
496	777	1273	64	19
371	316	687	76	8
801	78	879	54	9
289	553	842	70	8
3930	3439	7369	66	79

and institutional purposes; and two, that the pattern of analysis should focus on comparisons between different types of institutions within the system.

The content of the questionnaire, for upperclassmen and for alumni, was identical in most respects except for minor changes in wording and a few additions or omissions of items that would be applicable to one group but not the other.

The first section of the questionnaire consisted of activity scales dealing with a broad range of involvement in contemporary society and culture. Each of the activity scales contained from 9 to 14 items. The topics of these scales were as follows: community affairs, national and state politics, art, music, literature, drama, education, science (alumni questionnaire only), religion, intercultural affairs, and international affairs. The internal structure of each of the scales was the same, in that each scale included activities ranging from some which are relatively simple, commonplace, and easy to do, to ones which involve increasing amounts of interest, time, and commitment. The instructions for each scale were to "check each statement that describes an activity you have engaged in during the past year."

The number of activities checked in each scale provides a measure of the amount and depth of one's participation and interest. The number of different scales in which one checks more than some minimal number of statements provides a measure of the breadth of one's interests and involvement. Moreover, since many of the scales have certain roughly parallel items, one can derive additional indexes that have some relevance to the consequences or effects of higher education. For example, one can obtain a score indicating the number of different fields or topics about which one talks with his friends, an index of the number of different fields in which one has read a book, and the number of different fields in which one attempts to keep up with current events through the newspapers, magazines, or television. Thus the activity scales provide a rich source of information relevant to many of the intended or potential outcomes of higher education.

The second section of the questionnaire was designed to provide two kinds of measures: first, a measure of knowledge and awareness about certain major changes that may be taking place in American society, and second, a measure of attitudes toward such changes. In range of content, the various items dealt with changes in the labor market, the economy, the environment, education, science, government, industry, and other important aspects of the American scene.

The third section listed various educational objectives or benefits and asked the respondents to rate the extent to which the college experience was influential in the attainment of these objectives or benefits.

A fourth section was concerned with viewpoints about various social issues, particularly nationalism and self-sufficiency in governmental policy, the role of women, and civil rights with respect to minorities, free speech, and censorship.

The content of these first four sections may be viewed as criterion measures, that is, with activities and interests, attitudes and viewpoints, and estimates of progress related to a broad range of intended or relevant outcomes of higher education. The last two sections of the questionnaire dealt with the nature of the school and college experience and with a variety of personal information intended to throw light on some of the individual and environmental conditions that may help to account for performance on the various criterion measures.

With respect to school and college experience, items about college residence, major field, academic performance, participation in extracurricular activities, nature and extent of discussions with faculty members and counselors, aspects of the college experience that stand out in memory, and some corresponding information about the type of high school attended, high school achievement, and participation in various high school extracurricular activities were included.

The section dealing with personal information included the usual kind of census data such as age, sex, marital status, number of children, race, ethnic background, and occupation. It also included questions about personal and family background—economic, cultural, political, and religious. In addition, there were items inquiring about the various parts of the country in which the respondents have lived and about the extent to which they have traveled in other parts of the world. Finally, in the last part of this section, there was a brief personality test and a brief vocabulary test. The personality test items were related to four characteristics: theoretical orientation, complexity, autonomy, and anxiety. The vocabulary test called for definitions of words of various levels of difficulty.

From the scope of the questionnaire content and from prior comments about the college and university environment, it should be evident that our image of higher education as a nationwide enterprise was not one that saw it as many different institutions each trying to do the same thing and achieving some uniform goal with greater or lesser success. Rather we viewed higher education as a legitimately diverse enterprise in which certain kinds of institutions emphasize some goals to a greater extent than others and whose influences may be generally congruent with those differences in emphasis. This at any rate was our perspective and we shall be testing its validity as we present the results of our survey.

Information about alumni or about upperclassmen does not readily lend itself to proving that college caused their subsequent behavior and status in life or their current interests and attainments. Nevertheless, college graduates and college students, as consumers of higher education and former or current participants in the experience of higher education, are uniquely qualified to report on the benefits and influences of going to college. They have individually contributed to the quality of their own college experience and selectively consumed the variety of opportunities for learning and development which college made available to them. In this sense, it is inappropriate to consider them as educational "products" comparable to the products of a factory which receives and processes raw material. They were rather well-developed material when they arrived on the college campus, having some 18 or more years of prior development with all the cumulative experiences of inheritance and family, neighborhood, friends, church, and prior schooling. While college offers a kind of experience not offered by any other major institution in our culture, it is also for the person experiencing it part of a cumulative life history. One cannot separate education from all other experience in some cause-and-effect relationship. At the same time, an evaluation of higher education which ignored the reflections and subsequent lives of alumni or the interests and judgments of current students would surely be inadequate and incomplete. An exploration of patterns of association between college experiences, personal background, type of institution attended, and various student and adult activities, viewpoints, and characteristics can throw some light on how the diverse system of higher education operates in its natural setting.

Not all of the questionnaire content we have described will be drawn upon in the subsequent chapters of this book. For one reason, it is more than can be included in a relatively small volume. Also, some of it is redundant or overlapping so that not all of the separate pieces need to be included; and some of it is either irrelevant or unnecessary for the main purpose of the present report. Many items, useful for other purposes, do not empirically discriminate between institutions, and while we do not ignore all such items, we have concentrated our attention on institutional differences and the sets of items that best reveal the nature and extent of those differences.

In analyzing our data we have been guided by the following questions:

1. Are there differences between the eight types of institutions

    a. in the nature of the college experience reported by their students and alumni?

    b. in progress toward the attainment of various objectives and benefits on the part of their students and alumni?

    c. in the extent of student and alumni participation in civic and cultural activities and in viewpoints about various social issues?

2. Are such institutional differences today (class of 1970) larger or smaller than previously (class of 1950)? In other words, is there now more distinctiveness between institutional types (diversity in the system), or less?

3. What are the major dimensions along which institutions differ, regardless of type? And how similar or different are these dimensions as derived from the responses of the class of 1970 compared with the class of 1950?

4. To what extent do the major dimensions along which institutions differ also differentiate between the eight types of institutions?

5. Are there distinctive patterns of relationship between "input," environment, experience, and "outcome" variables?

6. Finally, are there distinctive types of institutions? What is the nature of their distinctiveness? And what is the past, present, and prospective "state of diversity" in higher education?

3. Institutional Differences in the College Experience

Each person's experience is unique in some respects and in others it is shared by all college students. Everyone attends classes, reads books, and takes examinations. Almost without exception the courses that college students take include some in the sciences, the social sciences, and the humanities. Beyond that, however, each student chooses a major field, and this choice provides a focus for a large portion of his academic experience. What he can choose depends on what is offered, and this in turn depends partly on the type of institution he attends. There are other important ways in which the college experience may differ. One might, for example, go to a college in which all or most students live in dormitories or in fraternities and sororities. This surely provides an experience that is different from attending college while living at home or in an apartment. The likelihood of becoming heavily involved in one or more sorts of extracurricular activities is no doubt also related to the amount of time one spends or can spend on the college campus as well as on one's personal inclinations. The data in this chapter examine these and other differences with respect to the nature of the academic experience and with respect to the nature of inter-personal experiences.

We begin by noting the differences among the institutional types in the proportion of their students who major in various vocational and academic fields. These data are shown in Table 2 for alumni and in Table 3 for upperclassmen. It is surely not surprising to see that most alumni, 76 percent, who attended colleges of engineering and science majored in engineering, and that most of those, 59 percent, who attended teachers colleges majored in education. These two bits of data simply confirm the validity of having classified such institutions as distinctive types. In the selective liberal arts colleges it is evident that the dominant academic culture is the social sciences and humanities. In the other liberal arts colleges this is also the largest single academic culture but there are also substantial numbers whose major field was either in business or in education or some other vocational field. In the

TABLE 2   College experience: percent of alumni in different major fields of study in college

Type of institution	Sciences	Social sciences, humanities, arts, languages
Universities		
SU	18	40
GU	17	26
SCOU	18	18
Liberal arts		
SLA	22	62
GLA	23	43
DLA	17	44
Other		
ES	13	2
TC	13	18
National baseline	17	31

TABLE 3   College experience: percent of upperclassmen in different major fields of study in college

Type of institution	Sciences	Social sciences, humanities, arts, languages
Universities		
SU	22	58
GU	15	33
SCOU	13	32
Liberal arts		
SLA	25	66
GLA	17	53
DLA	18	50
Other		
ES	21	20
TC	12	30
National baseline	17	40

| | Vocational fields | | | |
| | | Subtotals | | |
Total	Engr	Bus	Educ	Other
44	12	19	6	7
58	15	21	12	10
66	10	26	22	8
17	1	4	6	6
37	1	18	8	10
42	0	16	17	9
87	76	4	3	4
73	0	5	59	9
54	15	15	16	8

| | Vocational fields | | | |
| | | Subtotals | | |
Total	Engr	Bus	Educ	Other
19	7	4	3	5
51	9	13	17	12
52	1	10	29	12
11	0	1	3	7
30	0	9	13	8
30	0	11	8	11
59	41	6	4	8
51	0	14	37	5
42	8	9	16	9

universities, even the most selective ones, there are substantial numbers of alumni who had majored in engineering or in business. Especially in the state colleges and regional universities, the proportion of the student body whose major work had a distinct occupational orientation is substantial, namely 66 percent, with the bulk of those being divided between business and education.

For the upperclassmen, the pattern of enrollment in the major fields is similar. There are, however, a number of differences in the proportions between the alumni and upperclassmen reports. Some of these differences probably reflect changes in the status of certain institutions. For example, education is still the most common major in the teachers colleges; but compared with the alumni responses it is now smaller (37 percent *vs* 59 percent); and there is a higher proportion of majors in business and the social sciences, humanities, and arts. Few colleges are actually called teachers colleges today, and the higher proportion of non-education majors suggests the transformation of these institutions into emergent state colleges. A parallel indicator of this is evident from the somewhat larger percentage of education majors in the state colleges. A similar broadening of function has occurred in the colleges of engineering and science. In the selective universities the notably lower percentage of undergraduate majors in the vocational fields may be because what used to be available to undergraduates has now been moved up to the graduate and professional level. If the undergraduate data are at least approximately valid, one can conclude that teachers colleges and colleges of engineering and science are less distinctive or single-purpose institutions today than they were 20 years ago.

The second broad category of differences in college experience relates to the extent of involvement in campus life. We have used three indicators of this: first, residing on the campus; second, involvement in extracurricular activities; and third, the extent of conversations with faculty members and counselors. There is obviously a difference between a residential campus and a commuter school. In some schools located in the heart of a major city there are no provisions for student housing. At other colleges and universities nearly everyone lives on the campus. In both the alumni and upperclassmen questionnaires we asked where they lived during most of the time they attended college: a dormitory, a fraternity or sorority, at home with their parents, or in an apartment or some other place. To summarize this information, we added together those who said they lived in a dormitory and those who said they lived in a fraternity or sorority house. These percentages for each of the eight institutional types are shown in Table 4. The highest percentages of resident students are found in the various types of liberal arts colleges and the lowest percentages of resident students are found in the universities, with the colleges of engineering and science and the

TABLE 4   College experience: percent of alumni and of upperclassmen whose college experience was residential

Type of institution	Percent who lived in a dormitory or fraternity or sorority house	
Universities	*Alumni*	*Upperclassmen*
SU	46	57
GU	29	52
SCOU	30	57
Liberal arts		
SLA	80	90
GLA	60	86
DLA	54	70
Other		
ES	40	60
TC	52	59
National baseline	50	66

teachers colleges generally in between. It is probably not appropriate to make comparisons between the upperclassmen and alumni percentages on this table because the upperclassmen population is clearly biased in having more resident students than it should have, particularly in the larger institutions. There are two reasons for this: among the general universities and state colleges we do not have an appropriate number that are located in urban centers; and in the efforts made by the institutions to get a representative sample of upperclassmen, a better rate of response came in some cases from the resident students than from those who did not live on the campus. The consequence is that the differences between the institutional types are smaller for the upperclassmen than for the alumni data. Even so, the rank order of the institutional types is about the same in both samples, having a correlation of .90.

Amount of participation in extracurricular activities was not a usefully discriminating measure. Regardless of the type of institution attended there were about one-fourth to one-third of the respondents who said they participated "much" in two or more extracurricular activities, with generally higher percentages in the smaller institutions.

Another potentially important aspect of college experience is the extent to which individuals have discussions with faculty members and with counselors. The following question was asked of the alumni: "When you were in college did you ever discuss any of the following topics with a counselor or faculty member?" For the students, the

TABLE 5   College experience: alumni discussions with faculty members about various topics

| | *Percent reporting discussions at each type of institution* | | | | | |
| | *Universities* | | | *Liberal arts* | | |
Topic	*SU*	*GU*	*SCOU*	*SLA*	*GLA*	*DLA*
Academic work	59	59	57	75	68	67
Abilities and interests	35	37	38	52	48	48
Vocational plans	36	34	40	45	43	46
College plans	34	37	38	57	46	46
Personal problems	5	6	6	9	12	16
Financial problems	5	4	5	6	6	6

TABLE 6   College experience: upperclassmen discussions with faculty about various topics

| | *Percent reporting discussions at each type of institution* | | | | | |
| | *Universities* | | | *Liberal arts* | | |
Topic	*SU*	*GU*	*SCOU*	*SLA*	*GLA*	*DLA*
Academic work	62	64	73	64	74	72
Abilities and interests	50	49	52	52	55	54
Vocational plans	49	49	53	50	59	62
College plans	47	40	48	55	51	51
Personal problems	14	14	19	19	19	23
Financial problems	8	7	11	7	9	12

question was: "In college have you ever discussed any of the following topics with a counselor or faculty member?" Six topics were listed. Results for discussions with faculty members are shown in Tables 5 and 6.

It seems unlikely that nearly 20 years after the fact alumni would have checked any of these items simply on the basis of recalling a casual conversation. We assume that the discussions were of sufficient import to have been retained in memory. In Table 5 the data indicate that approximately two-thirds of the alumni reported discussions with faculty members about academic work. These proportions rise to 75 percent in the selective liberal arts colleges and drop to 57 percent in the state colleges and other universities. With respect to nearly all of the discussion topics the highest percentages are found among the alumni of the selective liberal arts colleges, and the lowest percentages are found among the alumni of colleges of engineering and science. Very

Other		National
ES	*TC*	*baseline*
59	59	64
35	44	43
29	40	40
30	32	41
4	8	9
3	6	5

Other		National
ES	*TC*	*baseline*
68	65	68
45	49	51
42	46	51
42	42	47
12	17	17
11	12	10

few alumni from any of the institutions reported having had discussions with faculty members about personal or financial problems.

Compared with alumni, the proportion of upperclassmen who reported discussions with faculty members about various topics are uniformly higher. This could be owing to the recency of the experience; or it could mean that faculty-student contacts are in fact more common now than they were 20 years ago; or it could be a reflection of the larger proportion of resident students in the upperclassmen data base. With respect to some of the discussion topics—academic work, abilities and interests, and college plans—the differences between the institutional types are not as great as they were in the alumni reports.

Reported discussions with counselors, by the alumni population (Table 7) and by the upperclassmen (Table 8), show that such discussions are less frequent than discussions with faculty members, and more frequent among upperclassmen than among the alumni when they were

TABLE 7   College experience: alumni discussions with counselors about various topics

| | Percent reporting discussions at each type of institution | | | | | |
| | Universities | | | Liberal arts | | |
Topic	SU	GU	SCOU	SLA	GLA	DLA
Academic work	34	33	33	40	41	29
Abilities and interests	27	28	26	29	34	26
Vocational plans	25	25	23	25	31	25
College plans	28	28	30	33	34	26
Personal problems	4	5	4	8	8	9
Financial problems	5	3	4	7	7	6

TABLE 8   College experience: upperclassmen discussions with counselors about various topics

| | Percent reporting discussions at each type of institution | | | | | |
| | Universities | | | Liberal arts | | |
Topic	SU	GU	SCOU	SLA	GLA	DLA
Academic work	44	53	57	38	52	58
Abilities and interests	35	38	43	31	59	47
Vocational plans	37	42	50	32	44	54
College plans	38	44	48	32	45	46
Personal problems	16	14	14	20	17	23
Financial problems	10	12	10	9	12	16

in school, with respect to most of the discussion topics. There are greater differences between the institutional types today than there apparently were some 20 years ago.

Another indicator of the nature of the college experience comes from responses to the following questions: for alumni, "What stands out in your memory about your college experience?" and for upperclassmen, "What stands out in your mind so far about your college experience?" Nineteen experiences were listed, with the respondents being asked to "check as many as apply." At this point we summarize the frequency with which two kinds of experience were cited: (1) academic—such as courses that opened up new interests, particularly stimulating lectures, professors who took a personal interest in them, encouraged them in their work, and helped them realize the demands of good scholarship and (2) peers—such as informal discussions with other students, living on the campus, social life, and extracurricular activities. From Table 9

	Other	*National baseline*
ES	*TC*	
28	27	34
21	21	27
17	20	25
20	20	28
4	4	6
5	4	5

	Other	*National baseline*
ES	*TC*	
62	42	51
41	31	41
40	33	42
43	33	41
16	12	17
15	14	12

one can see that there is little difference between the alumni and upper-classmen percentages, that the differentiation between institutional types is of about the same magnitude, and that the rank order of the institutional types is very similar (correlation .92), with respect to academic experiences. For experience related to peers the differentiation between institutional types is much greater in the alumni responses than in those of the upperclassmen. The relative lack of institutional diversity in the upperclassmen data may reflect the sample bias we discussed in reference to Table 4.

Experiences can be associated with many kinds of feelings. Most of what we have reported so far are the frequency of the experiences themselves—such as majoring in science, living on the campus, or discussing various topics with faculty members. Whatever the experiences may have been in different types of institutions, in the minds of the people who had them they no doubt add up to some degree of satisfac-

TABLE 9   College experience: types of experiences that "stand out"

| | Percent indicating different types of experience | | | |
| | Academic* | | Peers† | |
Type of institution	Alumni	Upperclassmen	Alumni	Upperclassmen
Universities				
SU	44	50	40	40
GU	44	50	29	43
SCOU	46	52	34	48
Liberal arts				
SLA	60	57	57	52
GLA	54	54	50	56
DLA	54	62	46	53
Other				
ES	37	40	28	50
TC	51	55	45	46
National baseline	48	52	41	49

*Percentage checking 3 or more out of 5 listed
†Percentage checking 3 or more out of 8 listed

TABLE 10   College experience: satisfaction with college experience

| | Percent who say they would "definitely" or "probably" go to the same college again | | Percent who say they would "definitely not" go to the same college again | |
Type of institution	Alumni	Upperclassmen	Alumni	Upperclassmen
Universities				
SU	78	78	5	5
GU	73	75	5	7
SCOU	78	67	5	9
Liberal arts				
SLA	76	72	5	8
GLA	73	64	7	14
DLA	75	72	7	8
Other				
ES	78	60	6	20
TC	72	64	5	12
National baseline	75	68	6	11

tion or dissatisfaction with college in general and the institution in particular. We asked both alumni and upperclassmen whether, if they could do it over again, they would go to the same institution, giving them four options to check their response: yes, definitely; probably yes; probably no; no, definitely. Table 10 reports the results. For the alumni, looking back nearly twenty years later, it seems to make little difference where they went to college, for three-fourths of them would go to the same place again, and very few had any definitely contrary feeling. For the upperclassmen, still in college, there are clear differences related to the type of institution they were attending. Least likely to go to the same place, if they could start over, are the students in colleges of engineering and science, the general liberal arts colleges, and the teachers colleges. In opposition to much popular mythology, it is the students in the large comprehensive universities (GU and SU) who appear to be most satisfied with their college experience.

Up to this point we have reported the percentages of individuals in different types of institutions who had various kinds of experiences, so as to give some specific information about relative frequency within types and magnitude of difference between types. The items that were selected for this purpose were ones we thought would be of most general interest with respect to difference over time (alumni *vs* upperclassmen) and to the distinctiveness of the eight types of institutions. We found that the differences between institutional types were smaller now (upperclassmen data) than previously (alumni data) in the following: the major field of study, campus residence, discussions with faculty, and memories related to peers. However, the apparent residential bias in the upperclassmen sample may account for some of this reduced differentiation. The difference between institutional types were greater now than previously in having discussions with counselors about various matters and in satisfaction with being at one's particular institution.

We turn next to another kind of analysis—more powerful in its significance and more empirical in its derivation. Instead of the composite response or average of all individuals from all of the institutions classified within a given type, we use for our analysis the composite or average response at each institution in our sample. In other words, rather than lumping the responses of 8,254 alumni and 7,369 upperclassmen into eight predetermined groups, we now represent each institution by its own average or mean score and then examine institutional differences directly. Before analyzing these institutional means, we eliminated two schools from the alumni survey and ten schools from the upperclassmen survey in which the response rate to the questionnaire was exceptionally poor. Because each institution is specifically identified (in the analytic procedure, but not by name) we felt that its own data base should be reasonably satisfactory so as to minimize any serious misrepresentation. For the alumni data, then, our analyses are based on N = 72 institutions, and for the upperclassmen on N = 69 institutions.

From the alumni and upperclassmen questionnaires we selected a common set of 35 items related to characteristics of the college experience. Applying the statistical procedure of factor analysis one can determine the major dimensions—that is, the item combinations or factors—along which the institutions differ from one another. The variables included and the resulting factors for the alumni institutions and the upperclassmen institutions are described below.

THIRTY-FIVE EXPERIENCE VARIABLES

1   Self-report of college grades

2   Residence: dormitory or fraternity-sorority

3-12   Major field of study
        Physical science or math
        Biological sciences
        Social sciences
        Language
        Humanities
        Arts
        Engineering
        Business
        Education
        Other

13   Highest degree attained (for alumni); plans to attend graduate school (for upperclassmen)

14-19   Discussions with counselors about each of six topics
        Academic work
        Abilities and interests
        Vocational plans
        College plans (choice of major, further schooling, etc.)
        Personal problems
        Financial problems

20-25   Discussions with faculty members about each of the six topics listed above

26-30   Participation in each of five types of extracurricular activities
        Athletics
        Creative (writing, drama, music, art)

Government and politics (campus government, political groups)
Social service groups
Academic groups (honoraries, departmental clubs, etc.)

31-34   Different kinds of experiences that stand out in memory
Academic (professors and courses)
Peers (student associations, campus life)
Independence (living away from home, being responsible for one's choices and activities)
Problems and difficulties (especially difficult professors and courses, having to work at a job and still keep up with studies, worrying whether one would really be able to graduate)

35   Satisfaction index (like college, would go to same college again, and regard college as very important experience)

From the intercorrelations of institutional mean scores of the 72 institutions in the alumni survey on these 35 variables, the items which best defined each of the five major factors that emerged[1] were as follows:

MAJOR
DIMENSIONS OF
COLLEGE
EXPERIENCE:
ALUMNI
SURVEY

Factor 1—Humanistic-social science-academic emphasis The experience elements in this factor are social sciences, languages, humanities, and arts as the major field of study; discussions with faculty members about college plans; academic experiences that stand out (professors and courses); and involvement in extracurricular activity related to government and politics. Negatively, the factor is further defined by not majoring in engineering and not having strong memories of problems and academic difficulties.

Factor 2—Involvement with counselors Five of the six listed discussion topics (all except the topic of "personal problems") had strong identification in this factor.

Factor 3—Faculty-counselor discussions of personal and financial problems The discussion of personal and financial problems, both with counselors and with faculty members defined this factor. It also includes extracurricular participation in social service activities. Just why this item should fall into the factor is not immediately evident, although it could be that social science activities often involve one in other people's personal and financial problems.

[1] Principal components solution, with varimax rotation.

Factor 4—Orientation to campus life   The items in this factor suggest an identification with campus living and association: residence on campus, memories that stand out related to peers, and memories related to independence and responsibility. The satisfaction index also contributes to the definition of this factor.

Factor 5—Involvement with faculty and academic experience   All of the discussion topics with faculty members (except the topic of financial problems) are in this factor, as are memories about professors and courses that were particularly stimulating. One other item, extracurricular activity related to campus government and political groups, also came into the factor definition.

There were a few other factors in the matrix, but they were such small ones, or so dubiously defined, that we did not include them in further analyses.

At first glance these factors may appear to be a rather odd and unexpected set of dimensions for defining institutional differences in the college experience. On second glance, at least three of them seem rather plausible—namely, the fact that institutions differ in their emphasis on the social sciences and humanities and arts (factor 1), on the involvement of students in campus life (factor 4), and on the extent of contacts with the faculty and the general stimulation of the academic experience (factor 5).

We note next the factors that emerged from the analysis of the same 35 experience variables for the set of 69 institutions in the upperclassmen survey. Along what major dimensions do institutions differ now?

MAJOR
DIMENSIONS OF
COLLEGE
EXPERIENCE:
UPPERCLASSMEN
SURVEY

Factor 1—Faculty and peer involvement   What defines this factor are discussions with faculty members about all topics except financial problems, memories that stand out related to academic matters (stimulating professors and courses), memories related to peer associations, and to the experience of independence.

Factor 2—Involvement with counselors   This factor is nearly the same as the similarly labeled factor in the alumni survey. It consists of all of the discussion topics with counselors except financial problems.

Factor 3—Academic emphasis and satisfaction   College grades, plans to attend graduate school, and the Satisfaction Index were three items in the definition of this factor. Also involved were participating in two sorts of extracurricular activities—creative (writing, drama, art, music) and social service. This seems to suggest a factor that combines academic success and satisfaction with some related extracurricular activity.

Factor 4–Academic and financial difficulties This factor appears to be a negative aspect of college experience. It consists of discussions with faculty and with counselors about financial problems and of events that stand out as academic difficulties (worrying whether they would really be able to graduate, trying to keep up with studies while also having a job, and encountering particularly difficult professors and courses).

Having identified the items forming each factor,[2] we then added them in proportion to their weight on the factor to obtain a factor score for each institution and converted these results into z scores–a normalized distribution of scores in which zero is the average of the distribution and 1.0 is the standard deviation. Thus each institution is located on a commonly defined scale according to its distance above or below the mean or zero point of the scale.

Figures 4 through 8 show the distribution of these institutional scores, based on the alumni data, for each of the five experience dimensions. The scores are plotted to show their location according to the eight institutional types. One can see graphically the extent to which institutions of any given type tend to have similar scores, and the extent to which there is a clear differentiation between the institutional types.

Figure 4 shows the experience dimension or factor labeled humanistic-social science-academic emphasis. Clearly, the likelihood of having a college experience with this emphasis is greatest in the SLA institutions and least in the ES schools. Except for the GLAs, which vary considerably among themselves, each of the types is relatively homogeneous. Note that occasionally one or two institutions are not enclosed within the bars. These may be thought of as deviant cases; they are shown as such so that the length of the bars encloses all or nearly all institutions of a given type. All the SLAs, and almost all the GLAs, DLAs, and SUs have scores above the mean; and all the ESs and almost all the SCs, GUs, and TCs have scores below the mean. There is nearly complete overlap between the SC, GU, and TC institutions; but for the most part the other institutional types are quite distinguishable from one another.

In Figure 5, *Involvement with counselors,* a very different picture is seen. Here there is great diversity within the types and little distinction

---

[2] All items had loadings of .40 or higher, with the median usually about .70.

between the types. Apparently the experience of discussions with counselors has little if any relationship to the type of institution attended.

Figure 6, *Faculty-counselor discussions of personal and financial problems,* shows considerable homogeneity within the SC, SU, and GU institutions, but also very clear differences between the DLAs and SLAs at one end and the SC, SU, GU, and ES institutions at the other. This aspect of college experience, then, has some relationship to the type of institution attended, although the GLAs and TCs are so heterogeneous that they do not constitute a definable type.

Orientation to campus life, Figure 7, varies considerably within each category of institutions, and results in much overlap between the several categories. Except for the SLAs, which are uniformly above the mean, all the other types have some institutions above and some below the mean.

In Figure 8, *Involvement with faculty and academic experience,* the distribution of scores produces almost a dichotomy between the typically above average scores of the SLA, DLA, GLA, and TC institutions and the typically below average scores of the SC, GU, SU, and ES institutions.

The corresponding distributions of institutional scores on each of the four experience dimensions that were produced by the factor analysis of the upperclassmen survey data are shown in Figures 9 through 12.

The first dimension, faculty and peer involvement (Figure 9), overlaps in content with the alumni factor that was labeled involvement with faculty and academic experience. Like its alumni counterpart, this factor discriminates between some of the institutional types, particularly the SLAs and GLAs at one end and the TCs, GUs, and ESs at the other.

The second dimension, involvement with counselors (Figure 10), is nearly identical to the alumni factor of the same name. Again, like its alumni counterpart, this upperclassmen experience variable reveals great diversity within institutional types and great overlap between types.

The third dimension, academic emphasis and satisfaction (Figure 11), discriminates clearly between SLAs at the upper end of the scale and the GUs, SCs, TCs, and ESs at the lower end. There is considerable diversity within the GLA, DLA, and TC categories, but institutions within the other categories are more homogeneous.

The fourth and last of the experience variables, academic and financial difficulties, from the upperclassmen analysis, is not a counterpart to the variable labeled faculty-counselor discussions of personal and financial problems from the alumni analysis. While both factors include discussions with faculty and counselors about money problems, the factor in the upperclassmen analysis is definitely linked to academic

(Text continued on p. 48)

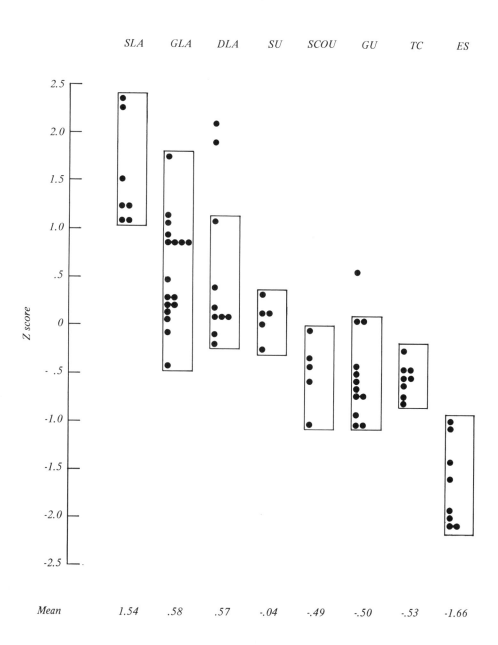

FIGURE 4   Differences in college experiences of alumni: humanistic-social science-academic emphasis

FIGURE 5   Differences in college experiences of alumni: involvement with counselors

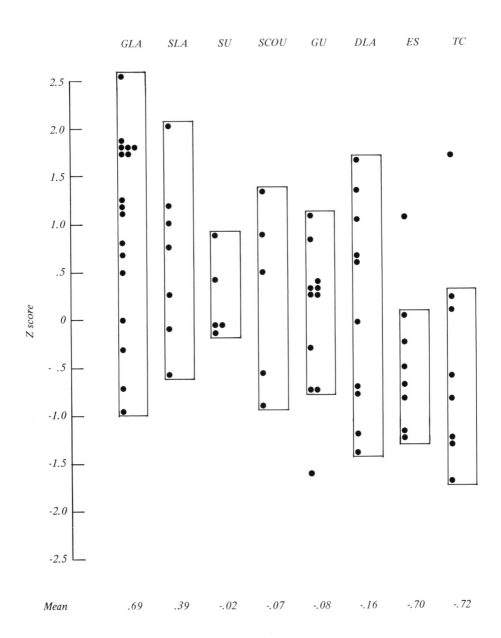

FIGURE 6   Differences in college experiences of alumni: faculty-counselor discussions of personal and financial problems

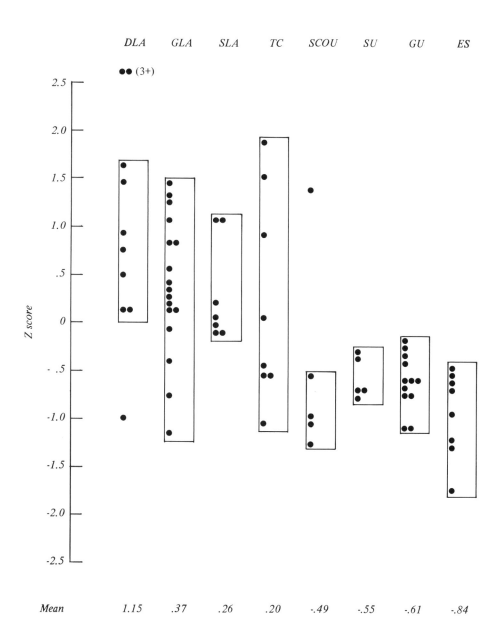

FIGURE 7 Differences in college experiences of alumni: orientation to campus life

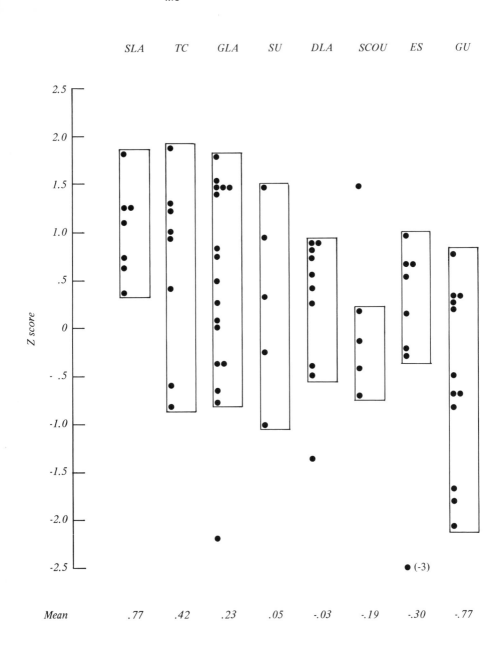

FIGURE 8 Differences in college experiences of alumni: involvement with faculty and academic experience

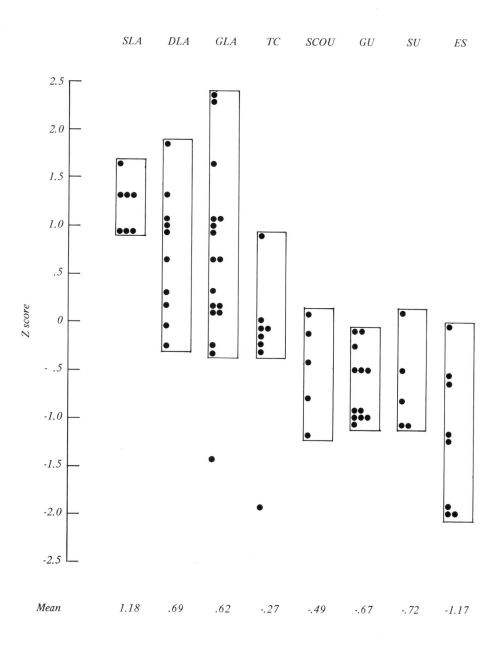

FIGURE 9   Differences in college experiences of upperclassmen: faculty and peer involvement

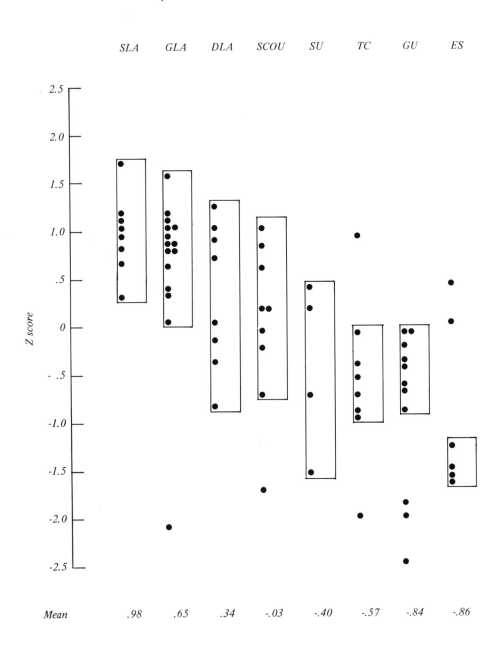

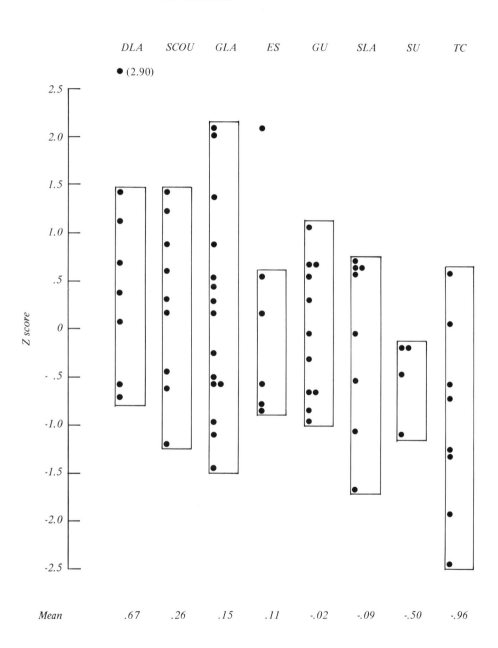

FIGURE 10 Differences in college experiences of upperclassmen: involvement with counselors

FIGURE 11 Differences in college experiences of upperclassmen: academic emphasis and satisfaction

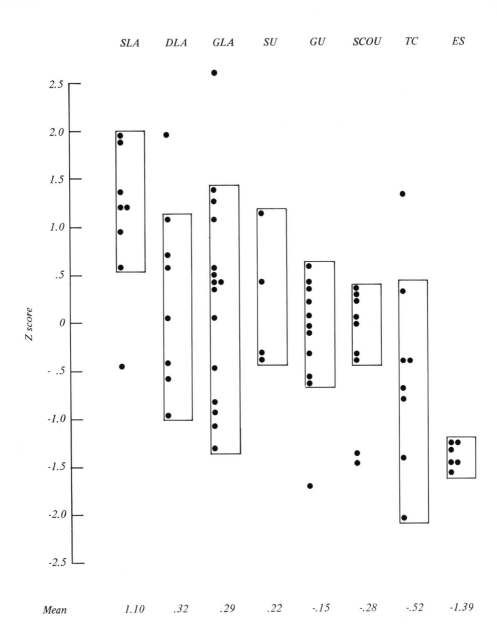

FIGURE 12 Differences in college experiences of upperclassmen: academic and financial difficulties

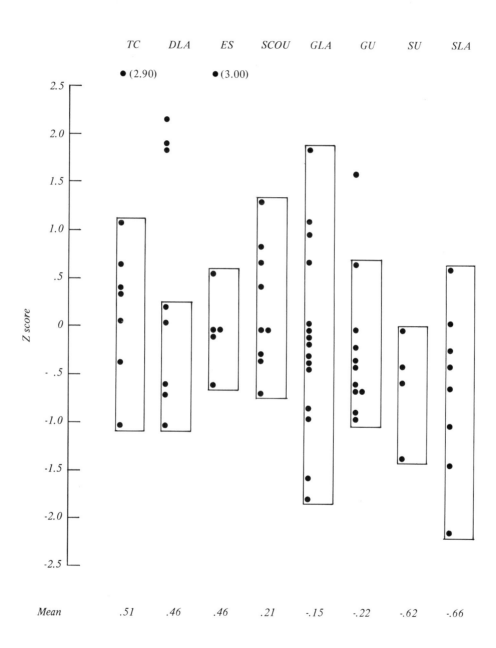

and study difficulty and worry whereas the alumni dimension is not so linked. In any case, the institutional differences plotted in Figure 12 reveal little systematic grouping according to the eight types and much spread within many of the types.

We can summarize the evidence from the alumni and upperclassmen charts on institutional differences in the nature of college experience by answering two questions: (1) is the diversity between institutions greater or smaller in 1970 than it was in 1950? and (2) are certain types of institutions more distinctive, or less, in 1970 than in 1950?

At the bottom of Figures 4 through 12, the mean z score for each category of institution was reported. In Figure 4, for example, the highest mean score deviates +1.54 from zero and the lowest deviates -1.66 from zero. Adding this gives a total deviation of 3.20. These total deviations are listed in Table 11. On the average, the deviation is greater in the alumni data than in the upperclassmen data.

To answer the second question we measured the difference between the highest and lowest institution in each chart (excluding deviant cases that were outside the bars). We then measured the length of each bar and determined how much of the total difference it was—that is, what proportion the range within a given type is to the total range. These percentages are shown in Table 12. The smaller the percentage, the more distinctive or homogeneous the institutions within a type are.

TABLE 11   Range of institutional differences on major dimensions of college experience

Alumni factors	*Range*
Humanistic-social science-academic emphasis	3.20
Involvement with counselors	1.41
Faculty-counselor discussions of personal and financial problems	1.99
Orientation to campus life	1.54
Involvement with faculty and academic experience	2.35
Average range	2.10
Upperclassmen factors	
Faculty and peer involvement	1.84
Involvement with counselors	1.63
Academic emphasis and satisfaction	2.49
Academic and financial difficulties	1.17
Average range	1.78

TABLE 12   Distinctiveness of institutional types on major dimensions of college experience

| | *Percent of total range in each type of institution* | | | | | | | |
| | *Universities* | | | *Liberal arts* | | | *Other* | |
Alumni factors	*SU*	*GU*	*SCOU*	*SLA*	*GLA*	*DLA*	*ES*	*TC*
1	16	25	23	30	50	30	25	16
2	26	50	55	62	83	71	33	48
3	16	27	22	35	70	43	38	81
4	64	74	23	38	67	36	33	69
5	27	23	27	18	61	48	45	30
Average	30	40	30	37	66	46	35	49
Upperclassmen factors								
1	59	26	53	41	47	62	15	29
2	22	44	58	53	78	49	33	69
3	39	32	20	34	66	51	10	54
4	34	41	49	66	90	32	30	54
Average	38	36	45	48	70	48	22	51

Looking at the average percentages, and ignoring relatively small differences, one finds that the SCs, the SLAs, and to a lesser extent the SUs, are less distinctive now than they were 20 years ago. The only large difference in the opposite direction is in the ES schools, which are seen to be more homogeneous or distinctive today than they were formerly.

On balance from the evidence so far, the conclusion is that there is now somewhat less diversity and distinctiveness in the system than there used to be with respect to various aspects of the college experience.

4. Institutional Differences in Progress and Performance

In this chapter we explore the extent to which there are differences in the kinds of benefits attributed to college by the alumni and the students of these different types of institutions, in their civic and cultural activities and viewpoints, and in other outcomes.

One section of the alumni questionnaire began: "In thinking back to your undergraduate experience in college or university, to what extent do you feel that you were influenced or benefited in each of the following respects?" The corresponding section of the upperclassmen questionnaire was: "In thinking over your experience in college up to now, to what extent do you feel you have made progress or been benefited in each of the following respects?" To each of the 17 statements listed below one could respond by checking "very much," "quite a bit," "some," or "very little." The statements are in the order in which they appeared in the questionnaire.

Vocational training—skills and techniques directly applicable to a job

Background and specialization for further education in some professional, scientific or scholarly field

Broadened literary acquaintance and appreciation

Awareness of different philosophies, cultures, and ways of life

Social development—experience and skill in relating to other people

Personal development—understanding one's abilities and limitations, interests, and standards of behavior

Critical thinking—logic, inference, nature and limitations of knowledge

Aesthetic sensitivity—appreciation and enjoyment of art, music, drama

Writing and speaking—clear, correct, effective communication

Science and technology—understanding and appreciation

Citizenship—understanding and interest in the style and quality of civic and political life

Appreciation of individuality and independence of thought and action

Development of friendships and loyalties of lasting value

Vocabulary, terminology, and facts in various fields of knowledge

Appreciation of religion—moral and ethical standards

Tolerance and understanding of other people and their values

Bases for improved social and economic status

In Table 13 the statements are abbreviated and rearranged in high to low order based on the percentage of alumni who marked them "very much" or "quite a bit." The corresponding percentages from each of the eight types of institutions are also shown. As one looks across the rows on this table one finds that for some of the educational benefits the differences between institutions are very small, but for others the differences are very great. The top four benefits listed in the table are ones in which the differences between institutional types are minimal. This is also true for the benefits related to social-economic status, and

TABLE 13   Educational benefits of alumni: national baseline and each type of institution

Percent of alumni indicating "very much" or "quite a bit" of benefit

Benefit	Universities			Liberal arts		
	SU	*GU*	*SCOU*	*SLA*	*GLA*	*DLA*
Vocabulary, facts	81	80	78	84	78	77
Critical thinking	74	71	68	77	69	72
Personal development	63	64	71	69	67	71
Specialization	63	62	59	64	60	65
Philosophy, cultures	68	59	61	81	73	73
Social, economic status	65	64	67	58	63	62
Communication	57	62	64	69	65	66
Literature	62	56	57	83	71	71
Social development	59	57	61	70	68	72
Individuality	60	56	57	74	66	64
Tolerance	56	51	54	69	63	71
Science	53	54	59	45	46	37
Friendships	50	45	52	62	56	69
Art, music, drama	44	36	38	70	53	57
Vocational training	38	43	53	24	33	39
Citizenship	34	32	40	43	43	42
Religion	19	23	23	36	35	74

to effective writing and speaking. No matter what type of institution the alumni attended the relative benefit seems to be about the same with respect to the acquisition of vocabulary and facts in various fields of knowledge, critical thinking, personal development, specialization for further scholarly work, improved social and economic status, and effective communication.

The benefits or influences which show the greatest divergence from one type of institution to another are ones related to religion, science, the arts, literature, and philosophy. There are also relatively large differences in the reported benefits related to social development, tolerance, friendships, vocational training, and citizenship.

Any deviation from the national baseline by 5 percentage points or more would be statistically significant, although in a practical sense it may not be highly important. We would guess that a deviation of 10 percentage points or more from the national baseline might have some educational significance as well as statistical reliability.

Other		National	Range of
ES	TC	baseline	differences
79	76	79	8
81	64	72	17
56	70	66	15
70	70	64	11
34	67	64	47
60	65	63	9
56	67	63	13
31	68	62	52
39	68	61	33
53	61	61	21
32	62	56	39
94	41	54	57
40	61	53	29
16	55	45	54
55	61	43	37
19	45	37	26
10	35	31	64
	Average range of differences		34

For the selective university alumni there is only one benefit, namely the lower benefit related to religion, in which the deviation from the baseline is 10 percent or greater. There are also negative deviations of at least 5 percent for the benefits labeled communication and vocational training. In the responses of alumni from the general universities there are no benefits in which the deviation from the national baseline is greater than 10 percentage points. However, the deviation reaches the level of 5 percent (all negative) on several benefits, namely, philosophy and cultures, literature, individuality, tolerance, friendships, arts, citizenship, and religion. Alumni from the state colleges and regional universities are 10 percentage points above the national baseline in their attainment of benefits related to vocational training, are above 5 percentage points on personal development and science, and below 5 percent on the topics of religion, specialization, and arts.

Alumni from the selective liberal arts colleges have many striking deviations from the national baseline. Their reported attainment of educational benefits related to philosophy and cultures, literature, appreciation of individuality, tolerance, and the arts are markedly above the national baseline; their attainment of benefits related to vocational training is markedly below the national baseline. On one other benefit—science—their attainment is below; on seven others—vocabulary, critical thinking, communication, social development, friendships, citizenship, and religion—their attainments are above, but by less than 10 percent.

The alumni from the general liberal arts colleges are moderately above the national baseline with respect to awareness of different philosophies and cultures, literature, social development, individuality, tolerance, arts, and citizenship. They are moderately below on science and 10 percent below on vocational training.

The denominational liberal arts college alumni are very markedly above the national baseline in their attainment of the benefit described as "appreciation of religion—moral and ethical standards." They are also substantially above the national baseline in their reported benefits regarding the formation of friendships, and of tolerance, social development, and appreciation of the arts. They are moderately above the baseline with respect to personal development, broadened literary acquaintance, and understanding different philosophies and ways of life. They are markedly below the national baseline in the attainment of benefits related to science.

Alumni from the colleges of engineering and science present a striking contrast. They are, of course, way above the national baseline with respect to the benefit related to science and technology. They are also noticeably above the national baseline with respect to the benefits attributed to vocational training, critical thinking, and specialization.

On many of the other benefits they are almost equally dramatically below the national baseline—for example, on those benefits described as personal development, philosophy and cultures, literature, social development, tolerance, friendships, the arts, citizenship, and religion.

Finally, the graduates of teachers colleges are seen as substantially above the national baseline with respect to the benefits of vocational training and arts and substantially below on the benefit of understanding science and technology. Moderate positive deviations are noted in specialization, literature, social development, tolerance, friendships, and citizenship. A moderate negative deviation is found on critical thinking.

Looking back on these differences in educational benefits one can clearly document the conclusion that the nature of the benefits claimed by alumni corresponds significantly to the nature of the institutions in which they spent their college years. For example, the benefit of vocational training is mentioned most frequently by alumni from those institutions in which the highest proportions of students had majored in occupational curricula, namely, the colleges of engineering and science, the teachers colleges, and the state colleges. Institutions having the most distinctive purposes, such as colleges of engineering and science and the strongly denominational liberal arts colleges, are precisely the ones whose alumni felt most benefited with respect to their understanding of science or their appreciation of religion. From colleges having the highest proportion of resident students we find the highest proportion of alumni attributing interpersonal benefits to their college experience, benefits such as social development, appreciation of individuality, tolerance, and friendships.

The corresponding results from the upperclassmen survey are shown in Table 14. It is immediately evident, from the high to low order in which the benefits are listed, that this order is quite different from that of the alumni. For the upperclassmen, the top five benefits are all related to personal and interpersonal matters, whereas in the alumni table four of the top five were related to academic subject matter. Of all the 17 benefits there were 3 in which the alumni national baseline percentage was substantially higher (10 percentage points or more) than the upperclassmen baseline: "vocabulary, terminology, and facts in various fields of knowledge," and "writing and speaking—clear, correct, effective communication," and "science and technology—understanding and appreciation." The upperclassmen percentage is substantially higher than the alumni on 5 of the 17 benefits: "personal development—understanding one's abilities and limitations, interests, and standards of behavior," "social development—experience and skill in relating to other people," "appreciation of individuality and independence of thought and action," "tolerance and understanding of other people and their values," and "development of friendships and loyalties of lasting

TABLE 14   Educational benefits of upperclassmen: national baseline and each type of institution

	Universities			Liberal arts		
Benefit	*SU*	*GU*	*SCOU*	*SLA*	*GLA*	*DLA*
Personal development	81	83	84	88	87	85
Tolerance	81	77	80	83	82	84
Individuality	81	76	74	85	81	77
Social development	71	74	78	80	79	73
Friendships	62	67	75	77	80	79
Critical thinking	75	74	67	78	69	73
Specialization	74	72	65	76	70	71
Philosophy, cultures	77	70	68	84	71	76
Vocabulary, facts	72	70	71	69	67	70
Social, economic status	51	62	68	49	59	62
Literature	65	55	55	76	64	62
Art, music, drama	58	50	55	69	58	59
Communication	44	50	52	52	46	50
Science	45	47	37	40	32	34
Vocational training	24	44	46	16	33	44
Citizenship	35	35	37	39	37	33
Religion	24	26	38	34	38	62

Percent of upperclassmen indicating "very much" or "quite a bit" of benefit

value." The fact that these personal and social kinds of benefits are claimed by higher proportions of upperclassmen than alumni may be owing to the immediacy of the experience, the greater number of resident students in the upperclassmen sample, or to a genuine shift in the value orientations of the more recent student generation.

More pertinent to our concern with institutional diversity is the clear indication that the range of differences between the institutional types is in nearly all cases smaller in the upperclassmen survey data than was reported for the alumni survey data. These differences are smaller, by 10 percentage points or more, with respect to the following outcomes: philosophy and cultures, literature, social development, tolerance, science, friendships, arts, citizenship, and religion. The average range of differences is 23 percent today (upperclassmen survey) compared with 34 percent yesterday (alumni survey).

The various objectives or benefits showing some noticeable deviation

| Other | | National | Range of |
ES	TC	baseline	differences
80	82	84	8
66	79	78	18
70	73	76	15
62	73	75	18
77	74	74	18
75	63	72	15
81	66	71	16
49	64	69	35
70	65	69	7
62	64	61	19
34	54	57	42
32	55	53	37
40	53	49	13
76	31	43	45
44	53	40	37
34	34	36	6
21	41	35	41
	Average range of differences		23

from the national baseline are as follows for each of the eight institutional types. Upperclassmen responses in the selective universities are 10 percentage points or more below the baseline for objectives labeled communication. They do not deviate above the baseline by as much as 10 percentage points on any item, but they are between 5 and 10 percentage points above with respect to individuality, philosophies, literature, and arts. The general universities and the state colleges do not differ from the national baseline by as much as 10 percentage points on any item, plus or minus. Smaller deviations below the baseline occurred on the objectives of friendships and religion for the GUs, and on critical thinking, specialization, and science for the SCOUs. Moderate differences above the baseline are also found for social and economic status and vocational training in the SCOUs.

Among the various types of liberal arts colleges, the GLAs are markedly below the baseline on science and moderately below on vocational training. They are moderately above on individuality, friendships, literature, and arts. The SLAs are markedly below on social and economic status and vocational training, they are 10 points or more above the baseline on philosophies, literature, and arts, and are above to a lesser degree with respect to tolerance, social development, specialization, individuality, and critical thinking. The DLAs are far above the baseline with respect to religion, and moderately below on science. They are also moderately above on tolerance, friendships, literature, philosophies, and arts.

In the other two types, the ES schools are high in science and specialization; the TCs are high in vocational training and to a lesser degree in religion. The TCs are also substantially below the baseline on science, and moderately below on critical thinking, specialization, and understanding different philosophies and ways of life. The ESs are below the baseline by 10 percentage points or more on six of the benefits—tolerance, social development, philosophies, literature, arts, and religion, and they are moderately below on individuality and communication.

We noted earlier that the range of differences between the institutional types was generally smaller in the upperclassmen sample than in the alumni sample. It is also true that the number of different objectives or benefits whose attainment deviated by 10 percentage points or more and by 5 percentage points, plus or minus, from the national baseline is smaller. Table 15 shows the number of such deviations in each type of institution, both for the alumni and the upperclassmen data.

In both time periods the colleges of engineering and science and the selective liberal arts colleges are seen to be the most distinctive although they are less unique now than formerly. The strongly denominational colleges have apparently lost some of their distinctiveness, as have teachers colleges. The selective universities are the only institutional type in which the number of deviations is greater for the upperclassmen sample than it was for the alumni sample.

Thus far in this chapter we have considered student and alumni self-reports of progress toward the attainment of various objectives or educational benefits. Another kind of outcome measure included in both questionnaires consisted of a series of checklists of activities. The extent to which people engage in certain kinds of activities is presumably a reflection of their interests, values, satisfactions and commitments. The content of the activity scales relates broadly to the content and emphasis of college study—namely, activities related to the social sciences, the humanities and arts, science, and, for some, religion. In the questionnaire the respondent was simply asked to check each activity he had engaged in during the past year. The number of

TABLE 15   Deviation from the national baseline in reported progress toward the attainment of various educational benefits

Type of institution	± 10 percentage points or more		± 5 percentage points or more	
	Alumni	*Upperclassmen*	*Alumni*	*Upperclassmen*
Universities				
SU	1	4	3	9
GU	0	0	8	2
SCOU	1	0	7	5
Liberal arts				
SLA	6	5	14	10
GLA	1	1	9	6
DLA	6	1	9	7
Other				
ES	11	8	15	10
TC	3	2	10	6

activities checked in each scale provides a reliable score or index of involvement in these civic and cultural affairs.

We report first the differences in the level of participation in various activities among the alumni of each of the eight types of institutions. These data are summarized in Table 16. Since the number of activities differs from one scale to the next, and activities in the different scales are not equally easy or hard to do, one cannot infer from the percentages that people are more interested, say, in literature than in art, but one can compare the responses of the different groups of alumni. In the table, each scale is identified, together with the definition of the level of activity to which the various percentages refer. For example, for the community affairs scale the national baseline for all alumni indicated that 44 percent participated in 8 or more of the 12 activities comprising that scale. Corresponding percentages for each of the eight institutional types are also shown. Insofar as possible, we selected for our national baseline the number of activities that came closest to describing the level of participation of 50 percent of the total group. By establishing the national baseline in this fashion we have provided a roughly comparable opportunity for the institutional types to vary from one another on each of the scales.

The percentages in Table 16 are portrayed graphically in Figure 13. In the charts the various types of institutions have been arranged in descending order based on the extent to which their alumni show greater or lesser participation in the activities in question. Deviations of

TABLE 16   Activities: alumni involvement in civic and cultural affairs

	Percent of alumni participating in various activities					
	Universities			*Liberal arts*		
Activities	*SU*	*GU*	*SCOU*	*SLA*	*GLA*	*DLA*
Community affairs: 8+ out of 12	40	40	44	50	47	41
National and state politics: 8+ out of 14	42	43	41	45	42	37
Intercultural affairs: 3+ out of 10	56	49	45	66	54	52
International affairs: 3+ out of 9	46	45	41	54	50	48
Art activities: 3+ out of 9	54	47	43	66	51	47
Music activities: 5+ out of 11	42	42	40	51	47	47
Literature activities: 4+ out of 9	54	44	41	62	59	58
Drama activities: 4+ out of 11	52	46	44	61	56	45
Science activities: 4+ out of 10	52	51	50	47	45	41
Religion activities: 7+ out of 9	37	46	44	38	46	72
Education activities: 7+ out of 10	37	37	39	46	42	44

5 percentage points or more from the national baseline are statistically significant. Deviations of 10 percentage points or more between any two types of institutions would also be statistically significant. It is apparent from the various charts in Figure 13 that alumni from the different types of institutions differ very little from the national baseline with respect to the level of activity in national and state politics. It seems to make little difference what type of institution one attended, for the subsequent level of political activity is about the same. On all the other activity scales, however, there are noticeable differences in the level of participation by the alumni of the different types of institutions. The greatest contrasts are revealed on activities related to religion, science, art, music, and literature. Despite the obvious difference in level of participation between institutions at the extremes of these charts, it is also important to note that in the middle ranges there are many instances in which the level of activity of alumni

| Other | | National | Range of |
ES	TC	baseline	differences
32	52	44	20
37	41	40	8
43	50	52	23
39	50	46	15
37	47	48	29
32	51	43	29
37	57	50	25
40	52	50	21
72	46	51	31
40	60	47	35
38	53	40	16
Average range of differences			23

from different types of institutions does not differ significantly. For example, on none of the activity scales is there a significant difference in the level of activity between the graduates of the general universities and the state colleges. And, except for activities related to religion and to a lesser extent for activities related to drama, there are no differences on any of the scales between the level of participation of the graduates of general liberal arts colleges compared with the strongly denominational liberal arts colleges.

In examining these various charts one can see again that there is a general congruence between the pattern of adult activities and the emphasis of the undergraduate college curriculum. For example, alumni from the colleges of engineering and science, selective universities, and general universities have the highest scores on activities related to science and these are also the institutions that have the largest proportion of alumni majoring in the sciences or in engineering. It is also

FIGURE 13 Activities: differences in civic and cultural involvement among alumni from each type of institution

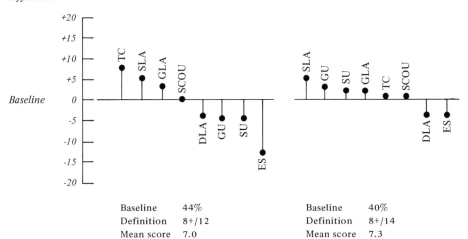

Community affairs

National and state politics

Baseline   44%
Definition 8+/12
Mean score 7.0

Baseline   40%
Definition 8+/14
Mean score 7.3

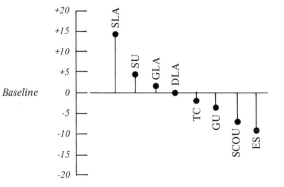
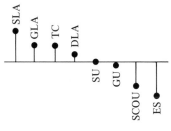

Intercultural affairs

International affairs

Baseline   52%
Definition 3+/10
Mean score 3.0

Baseline   46%
Definition 3+/9
Mean score 2.7

FIGURE 13 (continued)

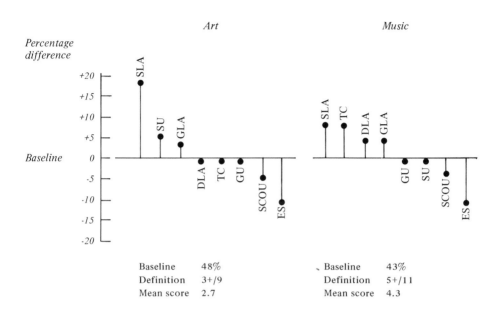

Art

Music

Baseline 48%
Definition 3+/9
Mean score 2.7

Baseline 43%
Definition 5+/11
Mean score 4.3

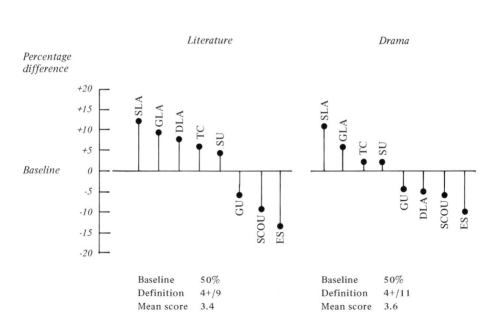

Literature

Drama

Baseline 50%
Definition 4+/9
Mean score 3.4

Baseline 50%
Definition 4+/11
Mean score 3.6

FIGURE 13 (continued)

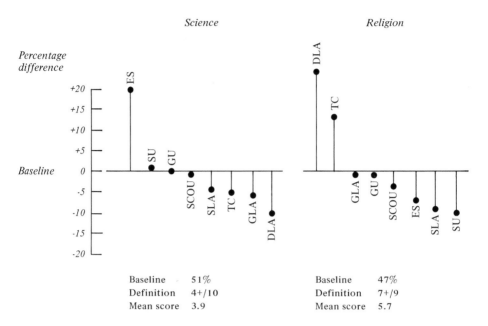

Science

Religion

Baseline   51%
Definition 4+/10
Mean score 3.9

Baseline   47%
Definition 7+/9
Mean score 5.7

Education

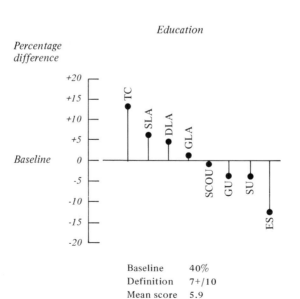

Baseline   40%
Definition 7+/10
Mean score 5.9

obvious that the highest level of activity related to religion was obtained by graduates of the strongly denominational liberal arts colleges. With respect to the social sciences, humanities, and arts, we noted in the previous chapter that the highest proportions of majors in those subjects were found in the selective liberal arts colleges. On adult activity scales related to these fields it was also the alumni from the selective liberal arts colleges that manifested the highest level of participation on nearly all of the relevant scales. A similar broad pattern of congruence is evident in comparing the results on the activity scales with the results on the attainment of various parallel educational benefits.

Responses to the various activity scales for the upperclassmen sample are summarized in Table 17. Note that the upperclassmen data included results on 9 scales rather than 11 and that in most of the scales the number of items is smaller. The scale labeled education was not included in the upperclassmen questionnaire because most of its content had to do with adult-citizen relationships with the public schools. Certain items had also been omitted from the upperclassmen questionnaire in the scales dealing with community affairs and national and state politics—omitted because their content was not appropriate for undergraduate students. Other reductions in the number of items resulted from statistical analyses of various scales with the subsequent decision to omit certain items in computing the scores. It was also partly for this reason that the previously separate scales on international and intercultural affairs were combined into a single scale in reporting the upperclassmen data. Since the number of items differs one cannot make direct comparisons between the scores of alumni and of upperclassmen. At the same time it does not in any way compromise the validity of comparisons between the various types of institutions. As in the alumni comparisons, we deliberately selected for a national baseline the number of activities that came closest to describing the level of participation of 50 percent of the total group, thereby providing a roughly comparable opportunity for the institutional types to vary from one another on each of the scales. If one compares the range of differences between the institutional types shown in the table for upperclassmen with the corresponding information in Table 16 for the alumni a number of rather large changes can be found. For example, on the scale of activity related to national and state politics, the institutional differences among the upperclassmen have a range of 28 points compared with a range of only 8 points for the alumni. This fact may reflect the intensity of political activism that characterized some campuses in the late 1960s. This is especially evident in the high scores of students from the more selective universities and liberal arts colleges. The strongly denominational colleges and the teachers colleges, where

TABLE 17   Activities: upperclassmen involvement in civic and cultural affairs

	Percent of upperclassmen participating in various activities					
	Universities			*Liberal arts*		
Activities	*SU*	*GU*	*SCOU*	*SLA*	*GLA*	*DLA*
Community affairs: *3+ out of 7*	43	36	39	36	35	28
National and state politics: *5+ out of 10*	52	45	34	59	39	33
Internat'l/intercult'l: *4+ out of 8*	57	43	36	69	48	42
Art activities: *3+ out of 7*	56	48	48	72	56	48
Music activities: *6+ out of 9*	53	47	51	62	55	49
Literature activities: *4+ out of 8*	56	52	49	67	57	46
Drama activities: *4+ out of 7*	60	53	55	64	56	46
Science activities: *3+ out of 10*	50	52	51	54	47	40
Religion activities: *4+ out of 9*	36	49	62	46	59	80

political activism was minimal, have correspondingly low scores. The combined international-intercultural scale for the upperclassmen sample shows a range of difference of 36 points between the institutional types compared with the alumni range on the two scales separately of 23 points and 15 points. Here again we find very high scores at the selective liberal arts colleges and universities where political activism was also most evident. The object of much activism internationally was related to the war in Vietnam and interculturally to racial discrimination. On two of the activity scales, science and music, the range of differences between the institutional types is much smaller in the upperclassmen sample than it was in the alumni sample. One suspects here that science has become a much more pervasive part of the general culture than it was in 1950 and that music may well be a more pervasive and therefore less discriminating part of the undergraduate collegiate culture than it is among older adults. The percentages in Table 17 are portrayed graphically in Figure 14. On the charts the various types of institutions are arranged in descending order based on the extent to which their upperclassmen show greater or lesser participation in the

| Other | | National | Range of |
ES	TC	baseline	differences
32	34	36	15
37	31	39	28
35	33	44	36
37	46	51	35
47	51	51	15
43	45	52	24
49	49	53	18
51	44	49	14
54	72	52	44

Average range of differences 25

activities in question, as was done in portraying the results from the alumni survey. Differences between the institutional types on the community affairs scale are relatively small. On the scale of art activities there is very little differentiation among institutions except at the extreme where there is a very large difference between the selective liberal arts colleges at one end and the colleges of engineering and science at the other. The scale of activities related to religion continues to show very sharp differentiation between the eight types of institutions.

Between certain types of institutions the differences on many of the scales are not significant. For example, there is not any significant difference between the GUs and the SCOUs on the scales of community affairs, international and intercultural affairs, arts, music, literature, and drama. The SCOUs are substantially higher than the GUs on the religion scale and substantially lower than the GUs with respect to activities related to national and state politics. In the alumni data, except for the religion scale, there were no significant differences between the GLAs and the DLAs. In the upperclassmen data, however, the GLAs were 10

FIGURE 14 Activities: differences in civic and cultural involvement among upperclassmen from each type of institution

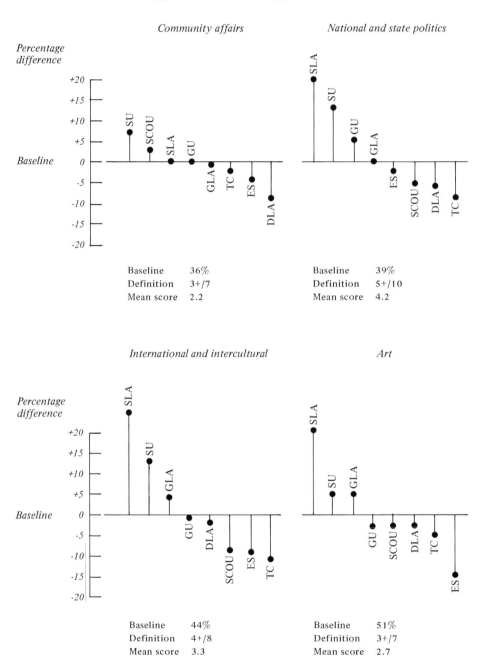

Community affairs

Percentage difference

National and state politics

Baseline

Baseline	36%
Definition	3+/7
Mean score	2.2

Baseline	39%
Definition	5+/10
Mean score	4.2

International and intercultural

Art

Baseline	44%
Definition	4+/8
Mean score	3.3

Baseline	51%
Definition	3+/7
Mean score	2.7

FIGURE 14 (continued)

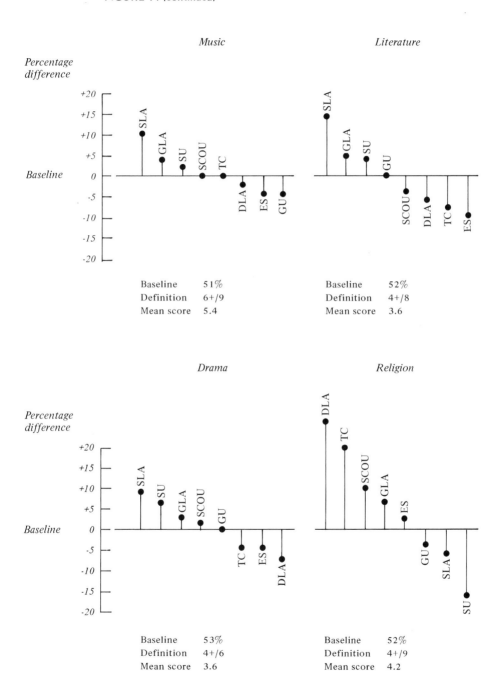

Music

Percentage
difference

Baseline	51%
Definition	6+/9
Mean score	5.4

Literature

Baseline	52%
Definition	4+/8
Mean score	3.6

Drama

Percentage
difference

Baseline	53%
Definition	4+/6
Mean score	3.6

Religion

Baseline	52%
Definition	4+/9
Mean score	4.2

FIGURE 14 (continued)

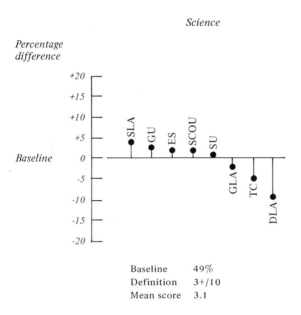

Science

Baseline 49%
Definition 3+/10
Mean score 3.1

percentage points or more higher than the DLAs in activities related to literature and to drama.

In comparing the alumni and upperclassmen data on these activity scales we do not find any general reduction in the extent of institutional diversity. While there is less institutional diversity in the upperclassmen data with respect to science and to music there is more diversity with respect to politics and to intercultural and international affairs. Overall the average amount of diversity between the two samples is almost identitical.

What do college students and alumni think about the society in which they are activie participants? What do they think about the desirability of certain directions of social change, and about some of the key issues of social policy? One section of each questionnaire was labeled *The changing society.* Under this heading we included a number of statements purporting to describe changes or trends that may or may not be occurring in the United States. We asked the respondents whether they thought there was such a trend, and, for some of the items, whether the change described would be desirable or undesirable, if it in fact occurred or was in the process of occurring. These responses were intended as a rough measure of social awareness and of attitudes toward certain directions of change.

For inclusion at this point we have selected a few of the statements to illustrate the nature of the content.

A new style of politics involving broader and more active participation at all levels is emerging.

More people are coming to realize and accept the value of self-expression, for example, through the arts.

As our society develops, the capacity for interdependence (relating with others) may be valued more highly than the capacity of independence and self-reliance.

Less importance is being attached to the value of individual success and achievement than has been traditional in our society.

Scientists and professionals are having an increasingly important influence on economic and governmental policies.

There is a tendency for large neighborhoods to become more exclusive in the kinds of people who live in them—white middle class suburbs as well as parts of the "inner city."

In Tables 18 and 19 the responses of alumni and upperclassmen to the desirability of these presumed trends are shown.

Alumni attitudes toward these social trends have little or no relationship to the type of institution they had attended. With respect to more participation in politics, 80 percent or more of the alumni from each of the institutional types agreed that this would be desirable. A similarly high proportion of alumni from all of the institutions felt that greater acceptance of the value of self-expression was desirable. High proportions of the alumni from each type of institution felt that it was desirable to accord scientists and professionals greater influence on economic and governmental policies. Roughly two-thirds of the alumni regarded as undesirable any trend there might be in the direction of greater segregation in neighborhoods, whether in the suburbs or in the inner city. The virtues of independence, self-reliance and individual achievement are strongly upheld by this generation of college graduates. Less than half of them think that it would be desirable to value interdependence over independence and self-reliance. This is particularly true for the graduates of the colleges of engineering and science, and is less characteristic of the graduates of teachers colleges. Only about one-fourth of the alumni think it would be desirable if any less importance was attached to the value of individual success and achievement than has been traditional in our society.

The corresponding responses from the upperclassmen sample, Table 19, reveal a very similar set of attitudes. In no case do the percentages for the national baseline differ by more than 5 points from the alumni percentages. Moreover, within most of the institutional types there are

TABLE 18   Social trends: percent of alumni regarding various social trends as desirable

Trends	Universities			Liberal arts		
	SU	GU	SCOU	SLA	GLA	DLA
More participation in politics	82	81	83	85	82	82
More value for self-expression	79	78	75	83	78	75
Value interdependence over independence	40	42	37	37	42	44
Less value on success and achievement	25	27	24	26	26	25
Scientists and professionals having more influence on policies	69	38	67	70	67	67
Neighborhoods becoming more exclusive (less integrated), U*	67	59	62	68	63	62

*U = "Undesirable"; all other items indicate percentage marking "Desirable."

TABLE 19   Social trends: percent of upperclassmen regarding various social trends as desirable

Trends	Universities			Liberal arts		
	SU	GU	SCOU	SLA	GLA	DLA
More participation in politics	86	74	77	84	79	79
More value for self-expression	83	72	81	86	83	84
Value interdependence over independence	44	39	41	43	42	55
Less value on success and achievement	35	21	23	35	24	29
Scientists and professionals having more influence on policies	68	60	62	70	62	60
Neighborhoods becoming more exclusive (less integrated), U*	83	62	53	80	68	72

*U = "Undesirable"; all other items indicate percentage marking "Desirable."

Other		National	Range of
ES	TC	baseline	differences
80	80	82	5
72	78	77	11
34	47	41	13
20	25	25	7
74	69	69	7
63	60	62	9
		Average range of differences	9

Other		National	Range of
ES	TC	baseline	differences
78	75	79	12
74	80	80	14
35	39	42	20
19	20	26	16
66	60	64	10
57	61	67	30
		Average range of differences	17

no differences even as large as 10 points on any of the items between the upperclassmen and alumni groups. In the few instances in which there is a difference of 10 points or more it is always the upperclassmen sample that has the higher percentage. The main contrast between the upperclassmen and alumni responses is the fact that on every item the range or spread of differences between the eight types of schools is greater for the upperclassmen sample. This difference is particularly strong for the statement about neighborhoods becoming more exclusive, where the spread is 30 percentage points—with 83 percent of the SU upperclassmen regarding such a trend as undesirable, compared with 53 percent of the SCOU upperclassmen.

Unlike the near unanimity of opinion among the different groups of alumni regarding the desirability of various social trends, and the general similarity of alumni and upperclassmen attitudes, we found a good many substantial differences between the various groups of alumni and between the alumni and upperclassmen in viewpoints about more specific social issues.

The social issues we have selected for inclusion in this report can be grouped under four headings. The first group is generally concerned with the theme of nationalism and self-sufficiency versus internationalism and cooperation:

We are not likely to have lasting peace unless the United States and its allies are stronger than all the other countries.

The United Nations should have the right to make decisions that would bind members to a course of action.

The United States has enough natural resources and scientific know-how to be economically self-sufficient.

The next two statements concern attitudes toward the role of women in contemporary society:

More women should be involved in policy formation both in business and in government.

Family patterns and attitudes should allow, and often encourage, married women to follow their own interests, even if they have young children.

The next two items measure attitudes toward the status of minorities:

If Negroes live poorly, it is in great part the fault of discrimination and neglect from whites.

More money and effort should be spent on education, welfare, and self-help programs for the culturally disadvantaged.

The final group of items is concerned with the issues of free speech and censorship:

People who advocate unpopular or extreme ideas should be allowed to speak on college campuses if the students want to hear them.

Literature should not question the basic moral concepts of society.

Responses of the different alumni groups to these social issues are shown in Table 20. The notion that peace depends primarily on United States military strength results in a division opinion close to the 40 to 50 percent mark among the alumni of most of the institutions. The major exception is for the alumni of the state colleges, where only 33 percent expressed disagreement with the concept of peace through strength. In general, two-thirds of the alumni agree with the notion that decisions made by the United Nations should be binding on its members. The lowest proportion of graduates accepting that viewpoint is from the colleges of engineering and science. The view that the United States can be economically self-sufficient is rejected by approximately two-thirds of the graduates from each of the eight types of institutions.

More responsible roles and greater freedom for women in society are endorsed by the highest proportion of graduates from the highly selective liberal arts colleges. Graduates from the colleges of engineering and science were least favorable toward greater policy roles in business and government for women. Graduates from the strongly denominational colleges were least agreeable to the notion that work and family roles should be compatible.

Slightly less than 50 percent of the graduates from the teachers colleges and the state colleges were willing to agree that the poor status of Negroes in our society is largely the fault of discrimination and neglect by whites. In contrast, 65 percent of the alumni from the selective liberal arts colleges felt that this was generally true. Most alumni agree that spending more money for the disadvantaged should be done. The range here between the institutional types was 60 percent of the alumni from colleges of engineering and science and 74 percent from the alumni of selective liberal arts colleges.

With respect to free speech on the campus, a little less than 50 percent of the graduates from the strongly denominational colleges, the state colleges, and the teachers colleges agreed that students should be allowed to hear speakers who advocated unpopular or extreme ideas. This contrasts with 75 percent of the selective liberal arts college alumni. As to the notion that literature should not question the basic moral concepts of society, nearly everyone disagrees, although the smallest proportion so disagreeing was among the alumni from the denominational liberal arts colleges.

TABLE 20   Viewpoints on social issues: percent of alumni holding indicated viewpoints

Topics	Universities			Liberal arts		
	SU	*GU*	*SCOU*	*SLA*	*GLA*	*DLA*
Peace depends on military strength (D)*	44	41	33	51	47	45
U.N. decisions should be binding (A)	64	61	63	70	67	64
U.S. can be self-sufficient (D)	62	62	61	62	65	58
More women in policy roles (A)	59	56	57	64	62	56
Work and family roles compatible (A)	74	68	71	78	73	63
Minority status fault of whites (A)	55	50	46	65	55	50
More money for dis-advantaged (A)	69	66	62	74	69	69
Free speech on campus (A)	67	58	46	75	65	48
Literature should not question basic moral concepts (D)	85	80	77	89	84	71

*A = Agree; D = Disagree

If one can regard viewpoints on all of these topics as tending either in a generally liberal or conservative direction, the results clearly indicate that the highest proportion of alumni having liberal viewpoints are those from the selective liberal arts colleges; the lowest proportions of alumni with liberal viewpoints are from the state colleges, the denominational colleges, and the colleges of engineering and science.

The upperclassmen responses (Table 21) show several major differences from the alumni. Sixty-four percent of the younger group disagree with the policy of peace through military strength, compared with 44 percent among the alumni; 86 percent of the upperclassmen support free speech on the campus compared with 59 percent of the alumni; and 76 percent of the upperclassmen compared with 67 percent of the alumni think that more money should be spent to aid the disadvantaged. Another noticeable contrast is the greater range of differences between the types of institutions on several of the viewpoints, particularly with respect to the statements about minorities, and the view about United States self-sufficiency. The only notable instance in which there was more diversity among the alumni was on the topic of

Other		National	Range of
ES	TC	baseline	differences
40	45	44	18
55	68	64	15
67	66	63	9
51	65	59	14
67	67	70	15
50	44	52	21
60	67	67	14
61	49	59	29
82	78	82	18
	Average range of differences		17

free speech. This is a result of the uniformly high agreement among the upperclassmen responses, where even the least supportive upper-classmen group (TC) is more supportive than the most supportive alumni group (SLA). Overall, the most liberal viewpoints among the upperclassmen are in the selective universities and selective liberal arts colleges, with the least liberal viewpoints in the colleges of engineering and science.

So far in this chapter we have reported the responses of alumni and upperclassmen from the eight institutional types to several indicators of educational progress and performance—progress toward the attainment of various objectives or benefits, participation in a number of civic and cultural activities, and attitudes and viewpoints about social trends and issues. All these can be regarded as measures of attainments, whereas the previous chapter was concerned with measures of experience. In some comparisons we found few differences between the institutional types or between the alumni and upperclassmen; in others, differences were substantial. Whether the items we selected to illustrate the content of the questionnaires are also the best items to define institutional

TABLE 21   Viewpoints on social issues: percent of upperclassmen holding indicated viewpoints

Topics	Universities			Liberal arts		
	SU	GU	SCOU	SLA	GLA	DLA
Peace depends on military strength (D)*	76	68	58	67	69	65
U.N. decisions should be binding (A)	70	66	65	66	64	68
U.S. can be self-sufficient (D)	55	58	65	59	61	50
More women in policy roles (A)	49	51	55	56	57	45
Work and family roles compatible (A)	73	64	70	71	66	54
Minority status fault of whites (A)	74	53	43	77	55	54
More money for disadvantaged (A)	88	74	71	89	80	78
Free speech on campus (A)	94	88	82	96	88	89
Literature should not question basic moral concepts (D)	97	90	84	99	88	88

*A = Agree; D = Disagree

diversity remains to be seen. For this purpose we need to look directly at the data from each institution regardless of type, and determine from factor-analysis procedures, as we did in the last chapter, the combinations of measures or factors along which the total set of institutions differ from one another. To do this, we selected from both questionnaires, a common (with minor exceptions) list of attainment measures as follows:

ALUMNI AND UPPERCLASSMEN ATTAINMENT VARIABLES

1-17   Educational benefit items, previously described

18-28   Activity scales (for alumni)

18-27   Activity scales (for upperclassmen) omits scale on education but includes international and intercultural affairs as two separate scales instead of the single combined scale previously described

29-36   Special activity scales (for alumni)

Other		National	Range of
ES	*TC*	*baseline*	*differences*
59	51	64	15
66	66	65	17
60	58	57	15
38	58	52	20
58	66	65	19
39	42	52	38
64	75	76	25
85	78	86	18
86	80	88	19

Average range of differences   21

28-36   Special activity scales (for upperclassmen)

Expressiveness—paint, sing, write, act, etc.

Critiques—read critiques of art, music, theater, movies, etc.

Contemporary arts—activities specifically referring to contemporary art, music, theater, novels, avant-garde movies, etc.

Breadth of discussion topics—number of different topics about which one talks

Breadth of reading—number of items checked that indicate reading books about various topics

Political involvement—selected items related to traditional political activities, such as party membership, volunteer work, campaign contributions, etc.

Community involvement—selected items such as neighborhood groups, community betterment activities, youth groups, support of the arts, etc.

Political activism—(upperclassmen only) participation in public protests or demonstrations about community, political, and international issues

(all these special scales are selected item combinations from the several activity scales)

37 Highest degree attained (alumni)

Plan to attend graduate school (upperclassmen)

38 Social trends items—awareness score

39 Social trends items—desirability score

40 Viewpoints items—score on items related to government

41 Viewpoints items—score on items related to role of women

42 Viewpoints items—score on items related to civil rights and minorities

43 Cosmopolitanism index—a combination of items including foreign travel, living in different parts of the country, and metropolitan living. This index is probably more meaningful for the alumni age group than for the upperclassmen.

44 Satisfaction index—this is the same index that was previously included as an experience variable, but it seems appropriate to consider satisfaction as a desirable outcome as well.

45 Vocabulary score

46-48 Personal traits items

    46 Autonomy (both alumni and upperclassmen)

    47 Anxiety (alumni only)

    47 Complexity (upperclassmen only)

    48 Theoretical orientation (upperclassmen only)

48 Number of books in the home (alumni only)

49 Occupational level (alumni only)—professional, semiprofessional, managerial, etc.

The factor analyses were made in two parts because the total number of variables, nearly 50, were too many to handle appropriately in relation to the total number of cases or institutions. One set of variables analyzed included the 17 educational benefits plus the 19 activity scores—variables 1 through 36. The other set included the same 17 educational benefits plus the attainment measures related to social trends, viewpoints, personal traits, etc.—variables 1 through 17 together with variables 37 through 49 (alumni) or 37 through 48 (upperclassmen). By using the 17 educational benefits items in both analyses we provide a common anchor for the results. This may be an advantage if one agrees that these items are of central importance and relevance. On the other hand, some of the factors produced by the two analyses inevitably contain common items because of this partially common content, and hence not all the factors are independent of one another.

From the factor analyses of the institutional mean scores in the alumni survey, nine factors emerged as follows:

Factor 1—Personal-interpersonal-humanistic benefits   All the items that define this factor come from the educational benefits section of the questionnaire. They include the humanistic benefits related to literature, philosophies, the arts, and religion, plus the personal and interpersonal benefits described as social development, personal development, communication, citizenship, individuality, friendships, and tolerance. The benefit related to understanding science and technology had a strong negative loading on this factor.

Factor 2—Social awareness and attitudes   The scores on the two scales related to social trends—the awareness score and the desirability score—plus scores on two of the viewpoints scales, namely those related to government and to civil rights, provide the main definition of this factor. Also included in the factor is the personal traits score for autonomy.

Factor 3—Intellectual-cosmopolitan   This factor includes the educational benefits items related to critical thinking and the acquisition of facts in various fields of knowledge, plus number of books in the home, the cosmopolitan index, the vocabulary score, and the personal traits measure of autonomy.

Factor 4—Vocational attainment   The educational benefits related to specific vocational training and to specialization and background for further work comprise part of the definition of this factor. To these items are added the highest degree obtained and occupational level.

Factor 5—Chauvinism-piety   This factor is defined by the educational benefits item "appreciation of religion—moral and ethical standards" combined with conservative scores on the viewpoints items related to government and to the role of women, plus a combination of personal traits indicative of low autonomy and high anxiety.

We used the word piety in labeling this factor because the item about religion was one of its defining elements. We used the word "chauvinism" because the viewpoints with respect to government are nationalistic rather than internationally minded, and the viewpoints with respect to the role of women tend in the direction of the attitude that women's place is in the home.

Factor 6—Critical thinking-knowledge-independence This factor is defined by three of the educational benefits items—namely, critical thinking, appreciation of individuality and independence, and the acquisition of vocabulary and facts in various fields of knowledge.

Factor 7—Civic and political activity Scores on the activities scales labeled community affairs, national and state politics, education, and political involvement define the nature of this factor.

Factor 8—Personal-social development, human relations, and community involvement All of the educational benefits items which defined Factor 1 also constitute a major part of the definition of Factor 8. To those educational benefits items, however, are now added a number of the activity scales—specifically, community affairs, education, music, expressiveness, and community involvement.

Factor 9—Humanistic-esthetic benefits and activity The educational benefits of broadened literary acquaintance, understanding different philosophies and cultures, and appreciation and enjoyment of art, music, and drama constitute part of the definition of this factor. To these elements are then added a variety of activity scales related to humanistic and esthetic topics. For example, art, literature, drama, the reading of critiques, interest in contemporary arts, intercultural affairs, current events reading, breadth of conversational topics, and extent of reading books.

Following the same procedure which we described in the last chapter, we obtained a weighted factor score for the institution on each of the nine factors and converted these to a standardized distribution in which the average is defined as 0 and the deviations above and below the average are defined in standard deviation units or z scores. The following nine charts, Figures 15 through 23, show the location of each of the 72 institutions in the alumni survey on each of the nine factors we have just described.

In Figure 15, showing the distribution of scores on the factor labeled "personal-interpersonal-humanistic benefits," it is apparent that there are substantial differences between some types of institutions and others, and that each institutional type is relatively homogeneous. There is almost total overlap between the SLAs, DLAs, and TCs. There

(Text continued on p. 92)

FIGURE 15 Differences in college outcomes of alumni: personal-interpersonal-humanistic benefits

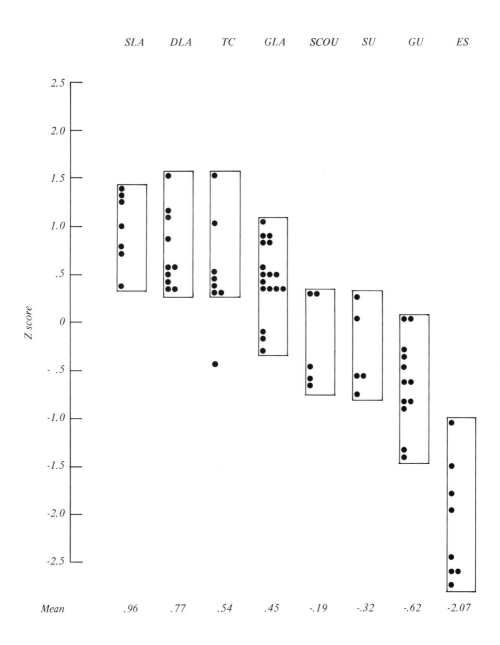

FIGURE 16 Differences in college outcomes of alumni: social awareness and attitudes

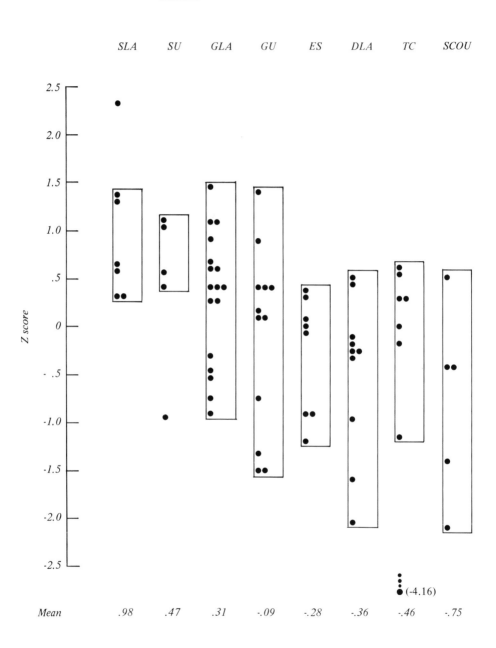

FIGURE 17 Differences in college outcomes of alumni: intellectual-cosmopolitan

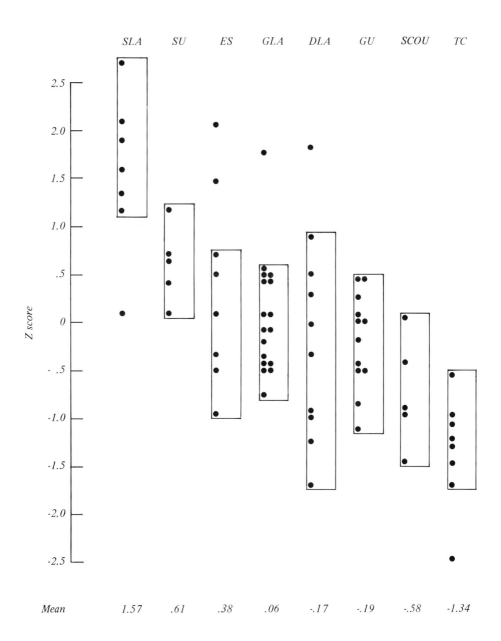

FIGURE 18 Differences in college outcomes of alumni: vocational attainment

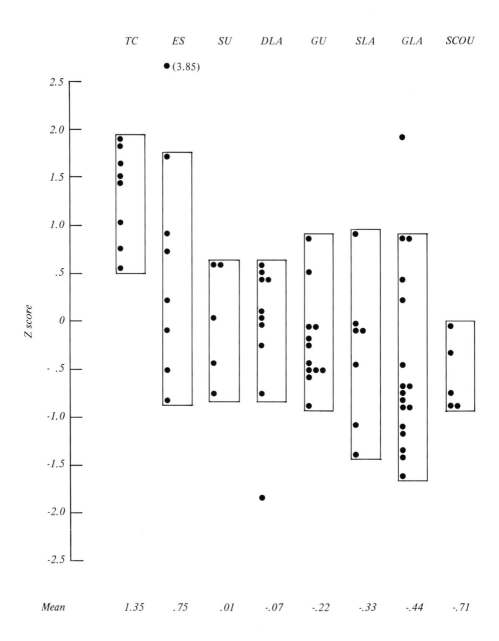

FIGURE 19 Differences in college outcomes of alumni: chauvinism-piety

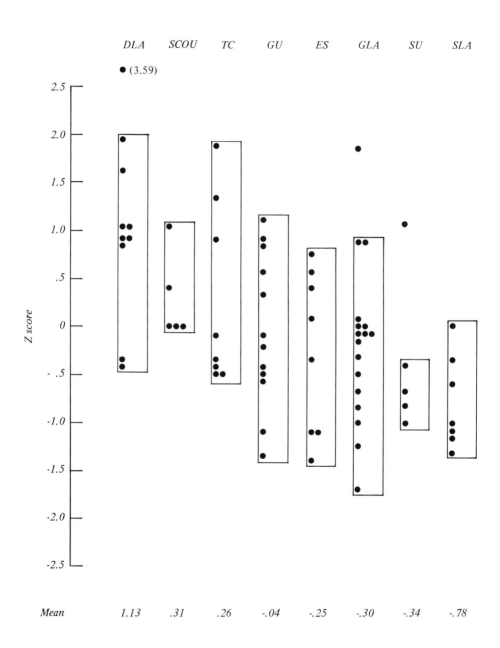

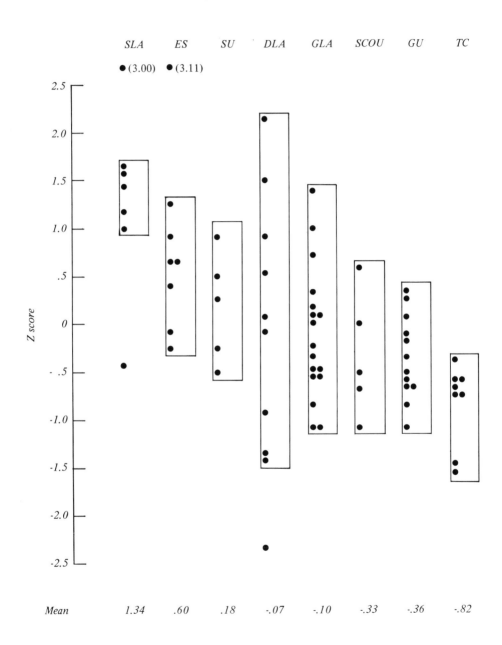

FIGURE 20 Differences in college outcomes of alumni: critical thinking-knowledge-independence

FIGURE 21 Differences in college outcomes of alumni: civic and political activity

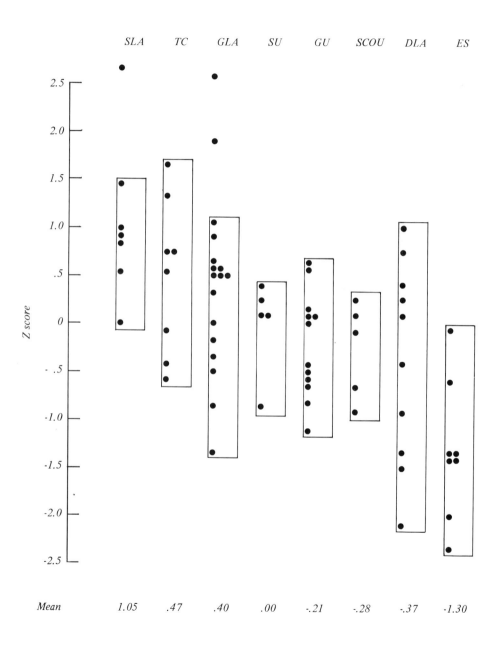

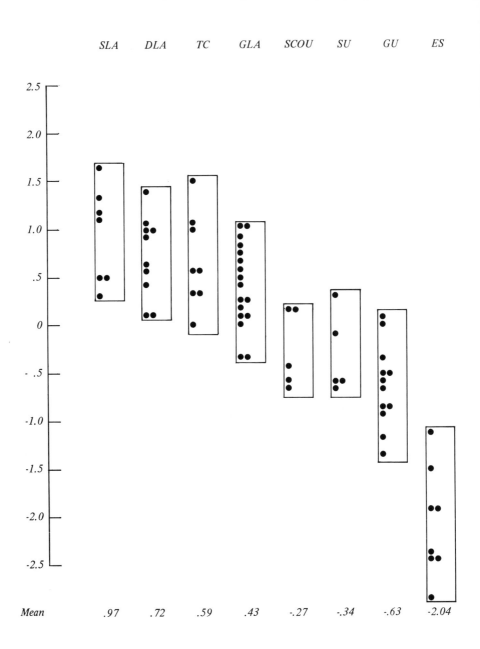

FIGURE 22 Differences in college outcomes of alumni: personal-social development, human relations, and community involvement

FIGURE 23 Differences in college outcomes of alumni: humanistic-esthetic benefits and activity

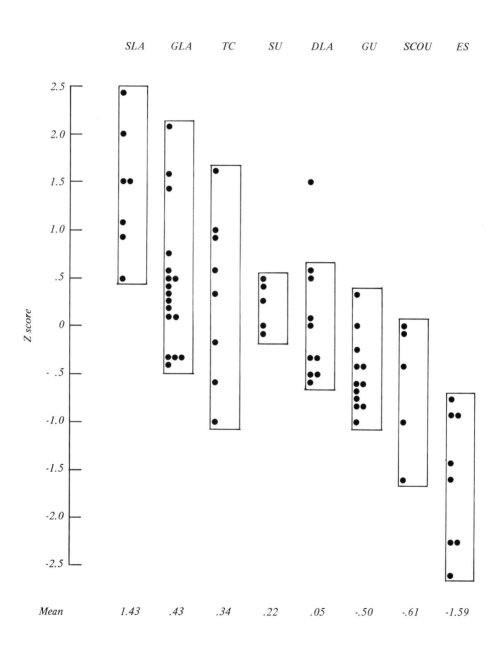

is almost total overlap between the SCOUs and SUs. At the extremes of the distribution, it is obvious that the SLAs, DLAs, and TCs are totally different from the general universities and the colleges of engineering and science. It is, of course, not surprising that the colleges of engineering and science should turn out to be relatively low with respect to humanistic benefits in contrast to the highly selective liberal arts colleges. In Figure 16, showing the distribution of scores on the factor defined as "social awareness and attitudes," the predominant feature of this chart is the rather wide dispersion of scores within many of the institutional types. There are great differences, for example, among the GLAs, the GUs, the DLAs, and among the SCOUs. With respect to the differentiation between types of institutions, it is clear that the highly selective liberal arts colleges and universities are quite distinct from the colleges of engineering and sciences, the denominational liberal arts colleges, the teachers colleges, and the state colleges. In view of the substantial overlap among many of the institutional types, it seems reasonable to say that attitudes with respect to the desirability of social trends and to viewpoints with respect to some important social issues depend not so much on the type of institution one attends as they do upon the particular institution one attends.

In Figure 17, which shows the distribution of scores on the factor described as intellectual-cosmopolitan, it is obvious that the selective liberal arts colleges are in a class by themselves. Almost all of them are higher on this factor than all or nearly all of the institutions in every other category. Most of the institutional types are fairly homogeneous, except for the denominational liberal arts colleges, which have a rather wide spread of scores. Clearly, the teachers colleges and the state colleges are at the low end of the distribution on this factor although there is substantial overlap among those institutions and the general universities, the denominational colleges, the general liberal arts colleges, and the colleges of engineering and science.

In Figure 18, the distribution of scores on the factor defined as vocational attainment shows that except for teachers colleges almost all other institutions overlap substantially with one another. The reason the teachers colleges are at the high end of the scale is owing to the fact that they have a vocationally oriented curriculum, that many of their graduates continue in school to obtain a master's degree for their teaching certificate, and that the second highest level in our occupational classification, described as semiprofessional, includes positions which ordinarily require a master's degree for entrance. Also in Figure 18, it is evident that there is a considerable dispersion of scores within the colleges of engineering and science, the selective liberal arts colleges, and the general liberal arts colleges. Whereas the teachers colleges, the selective universities, the denominational liberal arts colleges, and the state colleges are considerably more homogeneous on this factor.

In Figure 19, entitled chauvinism-piety, the first impression is that there is considerable overlap among all types of institutions. Even in the institutional type whose graduates are most chauvinistic and pietistic— the denominational liberal arts colleges, there is a considerable diversity among them. Some are extremely high on this factor and some are even below the average.

The factor described as critical thinking-knowledge-independence, portrayed in Figure 20, reveals a great deal of overlap among the institutions in the middle range but practically no overlap at the extremes, with the selective liberal arts colleges at the high end and the teachers colleges at the low end. Most of the institutional types, except for the denominational liberal arts colleges and the general liberal arts colleges, are reasonably homogeneous.

With respect to civic and political activity, the factor shown in Figure 21, there is again considerable overlap among the institutional types, while at the same time, there is a fairly clear differentiation between the extremes; the selective liberal arts colleges are at one end and the colleges of engineering and science are at the other. The diversity of scores is evident within the ES category, and even more so among the denominational liberal arts colleges; considerable diversity is also apparent among the general liberal arts colleges and the teachers colleges. The next chart, Figure 22, shows the distribution of scores on the personal-social development, human relations, and community involvement factor. It is certainly clear in this chart that there is a substantial difference between institutions at the upper end and those at the lower end. The selective liberal arts colleges, denominational liberal arts colleges, the teachers colleges, and the general liberal arts colleges, the state colleges and the selective universities are all higher on this particular factor than the highest institution classified as a college of engineering and science. The general universities are between those extremes. There is virtually no differentiation between the SLAs, DLAs, and TCs, and virtually no difference between the SCOUs and the SUs. At the same time it is interesting to note that each institutional type is relatively homogeneous in the sense that the spread of institutions within the type is not very great.

The last of the nine factors, labeled humanistic-esthetic benefits and activity, shown in Figure 23, again reveals a very sharp differentiation among many of the institutional types. Although there is some spread within the category labeled SLAs all of the SLAs are higher than all of the SUs, the GUs, the SCOUs, the ESs, and all but one of the DLAs. While there is a considerable spread of scores among the institutions classified as GLAs and TCs most of the other institutional types are relatively homogeneous with respect to their scores on this factor.

Looking back upon all of the nine charts, a number of conclusions seem to be warranted. The factor described as vocational attainment has almost no differentiation among the institutional types except at the two extremes. There is also a good deal of overlap among the institutional types on the factor described as chauvinism-piety and again, except for the extremes, on the factors described as critical thinking-knowledge-independence and civic and political activity. It is primarily on those factors that have to do with personal, interpersonal, humanistic and esthetic attainment measures that the greatest amount of differentiation is seen between the various types of institutions. It is usually the various kinds of liberal arts colleges that rank at the upper end of the distribution and the various kinds of universities including the colleges and universities of engineering and science that rank at the lower end.

Similar analysis procedures applied to the upperclassmen survey data produced six factors. The major dimensions along which institutions differed from one another are as follows:

Factor 1—Humanistic-expressive-active   The items defining this factor included, from the education benefits section, benefits related to literature, philosophies, personal and social development, esthetic sensitivity, individuality, and tolerance. To these items, were added the activity scores related to art, music, drama, expressiveness, contemporary art, intercultural affairs, and breadth of discussion topics. This factor is similar in a number of respects to the alumni factor labeled humanistic-esthetic benefits and activity.

Factor 2—Political involvement   This factor consisted of various items from the activity scales—specifically, activities related to national and state politics, to international affairs, to political involvement, political activism, and to the extent and breadth of topics about which one reads books.

Factor 3—Scientific-active   This factor consists of educational benefits related to background and specialization for further scholarly work, critical thinking, understanding science and technology, and the acquisition of vocabulary and facts in various fields of knowledge. Along with these benefits the factor also includes the science activity scale score.

Factor 4—Intellectual-liberal-independent   Along with broadened literary acquaintance and understanding different philosophies and cultures, this factor includes plans to attend graduate school, the desirability score with respect to social trends, liberal viewpoints scores on the topics related to government and to civil rights, the cosmopolitan index, the vocabulary score, and scores on the personal traits items related to autonomy and complexity.

Factor 5–Human relations Educational benefits related to personal and social development, esthetic sensitivity, individuality, friendships, and tolerance define this factor. Five of these six benefits were also part of the definition of Factor 1. In this case, however, no other items were included in the factor definition.

Factor 6–Scientific-theoretical This factor is identical to Factor 3 except that instead of the science activity score being added to the factor, the personal traits score described as theoretical orientation is added.

As in the previous factor analyses, weighted factor scores were computed and then converted to a standardized distribution of *z* scores. The resulting picture of institutional differences is shown in the next six charts, Figures 24 through 29.

Figure 24 shows a rather wide spread of institutional differences on the first factor, labeled humanistic-expressive-active. At the extremes all of the selective liberal arts colleges, all but one of the general liberal arts colleges, and all of the selective universities have scores higher than any of the colleges of engineering and science. There is almost complete overlap, by way of contrast, between the state colleges and the general universities. These results are surely in line with what one might expect, since colleges of engineering and science do not typically give much emphasis to the humanities and the arts.

Figure 25 shows the results on the factor labeled political involvement. On this factor also there are clear differences between institutions at the upper and lower end of the scale. All of the selective liberal arts colleges, all of the selective universities, and 8 of the 11 general universities rank higher than all or most of the institutions in the other categories. There is considerable overlap among the general liberal arts colleges, the state colleges, and the colleges of engineering and science. The teachers colleges also overlap to a considerable extent with those other categories but in general fall at a somewhat lower point along the scale. The high degree of political involvement that characterizes the more selective institutions and most of the large general universities is consistent with other studies of political activism among students in the late 1960s.

Figure 26 shows the distribution of institutional scores on the factor labeled scientific-active. On this factor, all of the teachers colleges and most of the denominational liberal arts colleges and state colleges fall below the midpoint in the distribution. In contrast, all of the colleges

(Text continued on p. 102)

FIGURE 24 Differences in college outcomes of upperclassmen: humanistic-expressive active

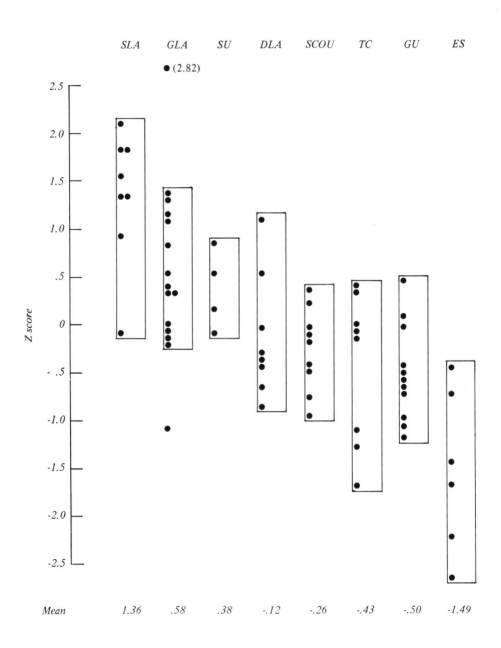

FIGURE 25 Differences in college outcomes of upperclassmen: political involvement

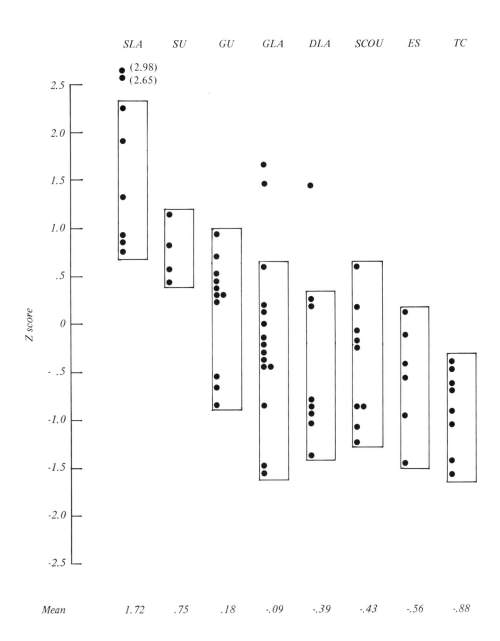

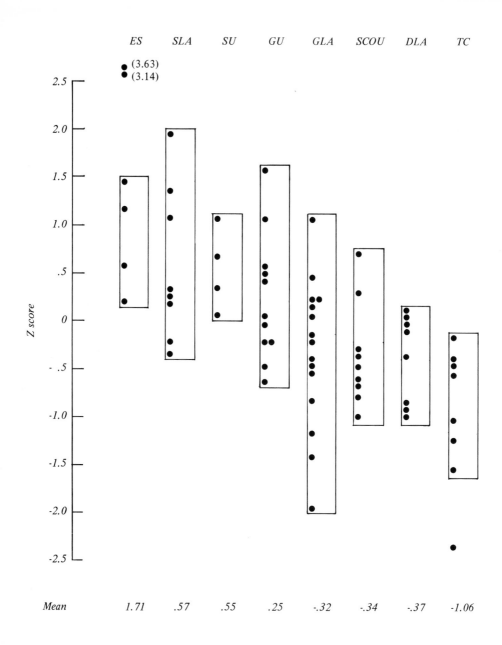

FIGURE 26 Differences in college outcomes of upperclassmen: scientific active

FIGURE 27 Differences in college outcomes of upperclassmen: intellectual-
liberal-independent

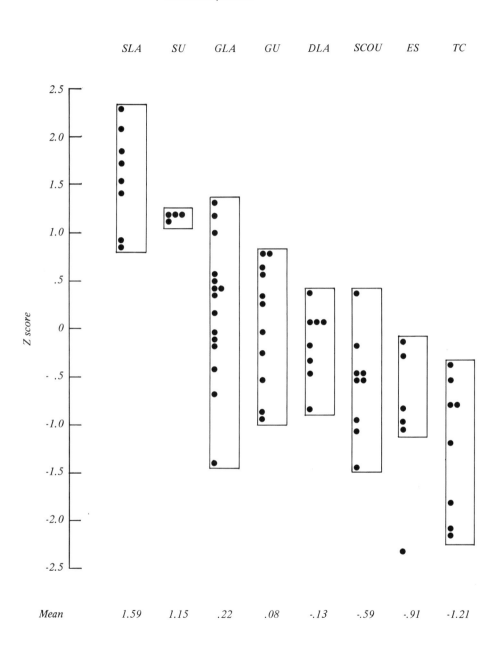

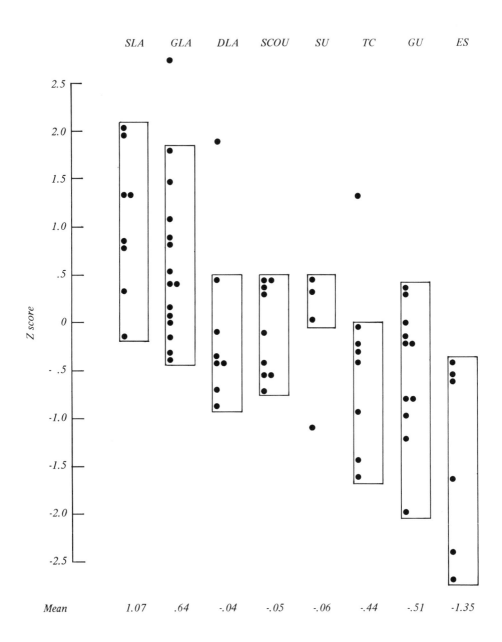

FIGURE 28 Differences in college outcomes of upperclassmen: human relations

FIGURE 29 Differences in college outcomes of upperclassmen: scientific-theoretical

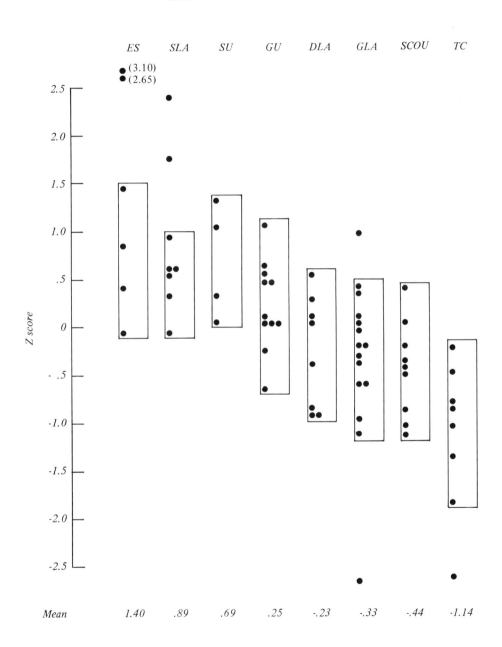

of engineering and sciences, all of the selective universities, and all but two of the selective liberal arts colleges fall above the midpoint of the distribution. There is obviously a great spread of scores among the general liberal arts colleges and to a lesser extent among the selective liberal arts colleges and the general universities. The other institutional types, relatively, appear to be more homogeneous.

The dimension labeled intellectual-liberal-independent, shown in Figure 27, again reveals that it is the more selective institutions that rank at the top of the distribution. Although there is considerable overlap between some of the other institutional types, a majority of the liberal arts colleges and general universities have scores higher than all but a few of the state colleges, the colleges of engineering and sciences, and the teachers colleges.

On the next factor, human relations, shown in Figure 28, there is almost no overlap between the selective liberal arts colleges and the general liberal arts colleges at the upper end and the colleges of engineering and science at the lower end. Only one of the teachers colleges and only two of the general universities rank above the midpoint on this factor. There is almost complete overlap between the denominational liberal arts colleges and the state colleges. None of the selective universities rank any higher than the highest of the state colleges.

In Figure 29, showing the distribution of scores on the factor described as scientific-theoretical, there is considerable overlap among most of the institutional types, with the exception of the teachers colleges, all of which fall within the lower half of the distribution, and the colleges of engineering and science, the selective liberal arts colleges, and selective universities, all of which fall in the upper half of the distribution.

To summarize the evidence for diversity and distinctiveness in outcome measures, as portrayed in the preceding series of charts, we followed the same methods described at the end of Chapter 3. Table 22 shows, for the alumni and upperclassmen data, the range of mean z scores on each factor. From this evidence, the range of difference between the types is seen to be somewhat greater for the upperclassmen that it was for the alumni. Perhaps more interesting, the magnitude of these ranges on the outcome measures is quite a bit greater than the ranges on the experience measures shown in Table 11. There is, in other words, greater institutional diversity in what comes out of the college experience than there is in the nature of the experience itself. Paradoxically, slightly reduced diversity in experience (class of 1950 *vs* class of 1970) has been accompanied by slightly increased diversity in performance.

TABLE 22   Range of institutional differences on major dimensions of progress and performance

Alumni factors	*Range*
Personal-interpersonal-humanistic benefits	3.03
Social awareness and attitudes	1.73
Intellectual-cosmopolitan	2.91
Vocational attainment	2.06
Chauvinism-piety	1.91
Critical thinking-knowledge-independence	2.16
Civic and political activity	2.35
Personal-social development, human relations and community involvement	3.01
Humanistic-esthetic benefits and activity	3.02
Average range	2.46
Upperclassmen factors	
Humanistic-expressive-active	2.85
Political involvement	2.60
Scientific-active	2.77
Intellectual-liberal-independent	2.80
Human relations	2.42
Scientific-theoretical	2.54
Average range	2.66

Table 23 provides an index of the distinctiveness or homogeneity of institutions within each of the eight types—the smaller the percentage the greater the homogeneity. The most heterogeneous group of institutions are the general liberal arts colleges; the most homogeneous group are the selective universities. The strongly denominational colleges, which were as heterogeneous as the GLAs in the alumni sample, are much less heterogeneous in the upperclassmen sample. There is a similar difference between the two samples, that is, toward greater distinctiveness within the institutions of a given type, for the colleges of engineering and science, the selective universities, and the teachers colleges. The only difference of five points or more in the other direction is in the selective liberal arts colleges.

In concluding Chapter 3 on institutional differences on college expe-

TABLE 23   Distinctiveness of institutional types on major dimensions of progress and development

Alumni factors	Percent of total range in each type of institution							
	Universities			Liberal arts			Other	
	SU	GU	SCOU	SLA	GLA	DLA	ES	TC
1	25	34	25	25	34	30	41	30
2	22	81	72	31	67	72	44	50
3	28	37	37	35	33	60	40	28
4	40	51	26	66	71	40	74	40
5	17	69	33	39	72	67	61	67
6	41	41	46	19	70	97	43	35
7	33	45	30	38	60	78	58	58
8	22	33	20	30	33	30	39	33
Average range	27	47	36	36	55	56	48	44
Upperclassmen factors								
1	21	35	29	46	35	42	46	44
2	21	46	49	38	56	41	44	33
3	28	56	44	59	77	31	33	36
4	4	40	40	33	60	29	22	42
5	10	49	25	45	47	29	49	33
6	35	53	47	32	47	44	47	47
Average range	20	47	39	42	54	36	40	39

rience we said that, on balance, differences between the class of 1950 and the class of 1970 revealed less diversity and less distinctiveness today than there was formerly. In concluding this chapter on institutional differences in progress and performance we find the opposite, for there appears to be more diversity and more distinctiveness today than there was formerly.

5. Ranks and Relationships

A simple way of identifying and summarizing how each type of institution is distinctive is to note the dimensions on which it has either a very high or a very low rank. Each of the eight types of institutions has been placed in rank order from one (high) to eight (low) on 36 measures from the alumni data and on 33 measures from the upperclassmen data. The number of measures is reduced somewhat from the total number we have previously reported. For example, we retained three of the five dimensions of the environment from the College and University Environment Scales. We reduced the 17 educational benefits to three categories—liberal education, vocational, and personal and social for the alumni data; and vocational, humanistic, and human relations for the upperclassmen—these reductions being based on factor analyses. We combined some of the activity scales into more general groups—art, music, literature, and drama into a single index labeled arts; and community affairs, politics, international and intercultural affairs (also education for the alumni data) into a single index labeled civic. We included the satisfaction index and the score on attitudes toward social trends among the upperclassmen measures, but not for the alumni because these measures were not usefully discriminating between the institutional types in the alumni survey. In the upperclassmen survey we combined the social viewpoints measures into a single index of liberal viewpoints. We included all of the experience and outcome dimensions from the factor analyses, and, for the upperclassmen, we added three combinations of major fields which had turned up as small factors but which we had not converted to z scores.

The institutional rank orders on all these measures are presented in Tables 24 and 25 for the alumni data, and in Tables 26 and 27 for the upperclassmen data. We consider distinctiveness as indicated by a rank of one or two at the high end and a rank of seven or eight at the low end of the scale, leaving the middle four ranks as indicative of non-distinctiveness. The following brief sketches of each of the eight institutional types summarize and compare the indications of distinctiveness based first on the alumni class of 1950 and second on the student class of 1970.

Alumni class of 1950

The highly selective university environment ranks among the top of the institutional types with respect to awareness, and the academic selectivity of its student body, but toward the bottom of the list in the extent to which the campus is perceived as a community. With respect to aspects of the college experience, the selective universities do not rank at the top of the list on anything. On the contrary, they rank low on the proportion of their alumni who claim to have had discussions with faculty members. On the various outcome measures, their alumni rank high on participation in activities related to science, in family income, in intellectual-cosmopolitan characteristics, and in their social awareness and liberal attitudes. They rank correspondingly low in their involvement in civic and religious activities, and in the extent to which they attributed vocational benefits to their college experience.

TABLE 24 Rank order of institutional types on specific environment, experience, and outcome variables, alumni data

	Environment				Experiences						
	Scholarship	Awareness	Community	College prone (selectivity)	Residence	Extracurricular activities	Faculty discussions	Counselor discussions	Memories-academic	Memories-peers	Vocational majors
Universities											
SU	2.5	2	7	2	5	5	7	3.5	6.5	5	5
GU	6	3	5	5	8	6	6	3.5	6.5	7	4
SCOU	7	7	6	6	7	7	5	4	5	6	3
Liberal arts											
SLA	1	1	3	1	1	1	1	2	1	1	8
GLA	5	5	2	4	2	2.5	3	1	2.5	2	7
DLA	4	4	1	7	3	2.5	2	6	2.5	3	6
Other											
ES	2.5	8	8	3	6	8	8	7	8	8	1
TC	8	6	4	8	4	4	4	8	4	4	2

Student class of 1970

From the more recent survey data, the selective university environment still emerges as high in awareness and student academic quality and low on its sense of being a community. These institutions, compared with other types, have more students who major either in the physical and biological sciences or in the social science and humanities, and relatively few who major in some vocational field. Despite the fact that relationships with peers do not stand out in their students' view of the college experience, the SUs rank at the top of the list on the index of student satisfaction with the institution. On the various outcome measures the SUs rank low on religious activities, vocational benefits, and human relations benefits. The scores of their students, however, rank them high in civic participation and political involvement, and in respect to various measures of intellectual, liberal, humanistic attainments. Out of all the 33 ranked variables the SUs are relatively distinctive on 19 of them. This compares with 13 out of 36 in the alumni sample. The selective universities have apparently become even more distinctive.

				Outcomes						
Benefits: liberal education	*Benefits: vocational*	*Benefits: personal and social*	*Viewpoints: government*	*Viewpoints: women*	*Viewpoints: civil rights*	*Income*	*Activities: civic*	*Activities: arts*	*Activities: science*	*Activities: religion*
5	8	6	4	4	2.5	2	7	4	2	8
7	4	7	5	5	5	4	5	6	3	3.5
6	3	5	8	6	8	6	4	7	4	5
1	6	1	1	1	1	3	1	1	5	7
2	7	3	2	2.5	2.5	5	3	2	7	3.5
3	5	2	6.5	8	4	7	6	5	8	1
8	1	8	6.5	7	6	1	8	8	1	6
4	2	4	3	2.5	7	8	2	3	6	2

TABLE 25   Rank order of institutional types on general experience and outcome factors, alumni data

	Experiences				
	Humanistic-social science-academic emphasis	*Involvement with counselors*	*Faculty-counselor discussions of personal and financial problems*	*Orientation to campus life*	*Involvement with faculty and academic experience*
Universities					
SU	4	3	6	4	7
GU	6	5	7	8	6
SCOU	5	4	5	6	5
Liberal arts					
SLA	1	2	3	1	1
GLA	2	1	2	3	3
DLA	3	6	1	5	2
Other					
ES	8	7	8	7	8
TC	7	8	4	2	4

GENERAL
UNIVERSITIES

Alumni class of 1950

The only distinctive aspect of the general universities' environment is its
large size. There is nothing distinctive at the upper end of the scale on
any of the variables of college experience. On the contrary, the GUs
rank low with respect to the measures of campus involvement, the
discussion of problems with faculty or counselors, and memories involving peers. On the various outcome measures the general universities are
not at the top of the list on any. They rank number seven, near the
bottom of the list, on attainments related to liberal education, personal
and social development, critical thinking-knowledge-independence, and
human relations-individuality.

				Outcomes				
Personal-interpersonal-humanistic benefits	Social awareness and attitudes	Intellectual-cosmopolitan	Vocational attainment	Chauvinism-piety	Critical thinking-knowledge-independence	Civic and political activity	Personal-social development, human relations, and community involvement	Humanistic-esthetic benefits and activity
6	2	2	3	7	3	4	6	4
7	4	6	5	4	7	5	7	6
5	8	7	8	2	6	6	5	7
1	1	1	6	8	1	1	1	1
4	3	4	7	6	5	3	4	2
2	6	5	4	1	4	7	2	5
8	5	3	2	5	2	8	8	8
3	7	8	1	3	8	2	3	3

Student class of 1970

The GU environment now ranks near the low end of the scale on community. The GU experience ranks low on faculty and peer involvement, as it did in the alumni results. The GUs, like the SUs, now rank high on the satisfaction index. With respect to the various attainment measures they rank high on only one—science activity. They rank low on the measures labeled social trends, human relations, and humanistic-expressive-active.

STATE COLLEGES AND OTHER UNIVERSITIES

Alumni class of 1950

The distinctive aspect of these institutions is their low ranking on the scholarship and awareness scales. With respect to the experience var-

TABLE 26 Rank order of institutional types on specific environment, experience, and outcome variables, upperclassmen data

	Environment				Experiences						
	Scholarship	Awareness	Community	B+ students	Residence	Faculty discussions	Counselor discussions	Memories: academic	Memories: peers	Vocational majors	Satisfaction
Universities											
SU	3	1	8	1	6.5	6	6	6.5	8	7	1
GU	6	3	7	5	8	7	5	6.5	7	3.5	2
SCOU	8	4	5	8	6.5	3	3	5	5	2	5
Liberal arts											
SLA	1	2	3	3	1	4	8	2	3	8	3.5
GLA	5	6	1	4	2	2	2	4	1	5.5	6.5
DLA	4	5	2	6	3	1	1	1	2	5.5	3.5
Other											
ES	2	8	4	2	4	8	4	8	4	1	8
TC	7	7	6	7	5	5	7	3	6	3.5	6.5

iables they rank low on the measure of campus involvement, and they do not rank high on any. On the outcome measures they are not found among the top ranks on any of the variables except for chauvinism-piety. They are at or near the lowest rank with respect to the proportion of their alumni having social awareness and liberal viewpoints, and proportion of their alumni participating in activities related to the arts, or to humanistic-esthetic attainments. They are also at the low end of the rank order on the measure of vocational attainment.

Student class of 1970

The SCOU environment no longer ranks low in respect to awareness, but it remains at the low end of the scale on scholarship and the proportion of academic achievers in the student body. Among the college experience variables the SCOUs rank high in their proportion of vocational majors and in involvement with counselors, and low in the proportion of majors in physical and biological sciences. On the various outcome measures they rank high on human relations benefits and low on science-theoretical matters. Of all the institutional types, the state

Benefits: vocational	Benefits: humanistic	Benefits: human relations	Social trends	Liberal viewpoints	Activities: civic	Activities: arts	Activities: science	Activities: religion
				Outcomes				
7	2	7	2	2	1	3	5	8
3.5	5	6	7	4	3	5	2	6
3.5	6	1	5	5	5	4	3.5	3
8	1	3	1	1	2	1	1	7
6	4	4	4	3	4	2	6	4
5	3	2	3	6	7	6.5	8	1
1	8	8	6	8	6	8	3.5	5
2	7	5	8	7	8	6.5	7	2

colleges have the fewest distinguishing characteristics—ranking at one end or the other, rather than in the middle, on 7 of the 33 measures.

SELECTIVE LIBERAL ARTS COLLEGES

Alumni class of 1950

In nearly all respects these are among the most distinctive of the eight types of institutions in our study. They rank high on scholarship, awareness, and the academic selectivity of their student body. The alumni of these institutions reported considerable involvement in campus activities, in discussions with faculty members and counselors, and in memories related both to the academic life and to the student life. They rank at the bottom of the list with respect to the proportion of their students who majored in vocational subjects. On the various outcome measures they rank number one on benefits related to liberal education and personal and social development, liberal viewpoints on social issues, involvement in activities related to civic and political affairs and the arts. They rank low on their involvement in activities related to religion, and on the characteristic labeled chauvinism-piety.

TABLE 27   Rank order of institutional types on general experience and outcome factors, upperclassmen data

	Experiences						
	Faculty and peer involvement	*Academic emphasis and satisfaction*	*Involvement with counselors*	*Academic and financial difficulties*	*Language and arts majors*	*Social science and humanities majors*	*Physical and biological science majors*
Universities							
SU	5	4	7	7	5	2	2
GU	7	5	5	6	6.5	5	6
SCOU	4	6	2	4	6.5	6	7
Liberal arts							
SLA	1	1	6	8	4	1	1
GLA	2	3	3	5	1.5	3	5
DLA	3	2	1	2.5	3	4	4
Other							
ES	8	8	4	2.5	8	8	3
TC	6	7	8	1	1.5	7	8

Student class of 1970

These institutions are still characterized by top ranks on scholarship
and awareness, on faculty and peer involvement, and academic involvement and satisfaction. They do not rank high on conversations with
counselors, as they did in the alumni data; instead, they now fall at the
bottom of the rank order. They have, proportionately, the fewest vocational majors and the most in science, social science and humanities. On
the outcome measures they rank at or next to the top on everything
except vocational benefits and religious activities. So, our data indicate
that these institutions have retained their status as a highly distinctive
type—being at one end or the other of the rank order on 25 of the 33
measures.

	Outcomes				
Humanistic-expressive-active	*Political involvement*	*Scientific-active*	*Intellectual-liberal-independent*	*Human relations*	*Scientific-theoretical*
3	2	3	2	5	3
7	3	4	4	7	4
5	6	6	6	4	7
1	1	2	1	1	2
2	4	5	3	2	6
4	5	7	5	3	5
8	7	1	7	8	1
6	8	8	8	6	8

GENERAL LIBERAL ARTS COLLEGES

Alumni class of 1950

These institutions have an environment characterized by a strong sense of community, but otherwise are not distinctive. Their alumni reported a high level of involvement in campus affairs, in discussions with counselors, in memories related to student affairs, and in a setting with both humanistic and academic emphasis. A small proportion of the alumni, compared with those from other institutions, had majored in vocational subjects. On the outcome measures they rank high on benefits related to liberal education, on liberal viewpoint with respect to government, on activities related to the arts, and to humanistic-esthetic concerns. They rank correspondingly low on vocational benefits attributed to the college experience, and on their participation in activities related to science.

Student class of 1970

On the evidence from the upperclassmen reports, these institutions are still characterized as friendly communities. And the college experience is still characterized by high rank, among the eight types, with respect to faculty and peer and campus involvement. The GLAs also rank high in the proportion of majors in arts and languages. On the outcome measures, they rank high with respect to humanistic-expressive, human relations, and art related activities. They are not at the low end of the rank order on any of the outcome variables. The GLAs today appear at the ends of the rank order on fewer indicators than they did in the alumni report—10 out of 33 now, 15 out of 36 formerly.

DENOMINATIONAL LIBERAL ARTS COLLEGES

Alumni class of 1950

These institutions also emerge as fairly distinctive. They rank high on the community aspect of the college environment and they are of course among the smallest institutions in size. Their alumni report considerable discussions with faculty members and with both faculty and counselors about personal problems. They rank high with respect to attainment of personal and social benefits, human relations benefits, chauvinism-piety, and the extent of their participation in activities related to religion. They are correspondingly low in the proportion of their alumni holding liberal viewpoints about the role of women, in their involvement in activities related to science, civic and political activity, and in their income.

Student class of 1970

The feeling of community, both in the environment and in the nature of the college experience, is still strong in these institutions. They rank high on conversations with faculty and with counselors, and on academic experiences and peer experiences that stand out. On the outcome measures they rank high on human relations benefits and highest of all on activities related to religion. Their primary distinctiveness remains their religious character. In other respects they are much closer today to the general liberal arts colleges than they were formerly. In the alumni rankings they differed by three ranks or more from the GLAs on 12 of the measures; in the upperclassmen data differences of that magnitude are found on 6 of the measures.

COLLEGES OF ENGINEERING AND SCIENCE

Alumni class of 1950

These institutions have an environment that is strong on scholarship but weak on awareness and community. They rank at the bottom or next to the bottom on all the measures of college experience that involve interpersonal relationships. They rank at the top of the list on the proportion of their alumni who had majored in vocational fields. On the outcome measures they rank at the top in benefits related to vocational training, in activities related to science, and to income, and next to the top in the outcome measure labeled critical thinking-knowledge-independence. In contrast, they are at the bottom of the rank order on benefits related to liberal education and personal and social development, and on the involvement of their alumni in activities related to civic and political affairs, and to the arts and other humanistic outcomes.

Student class of 1970

From the upperclassmen data the ES environment is still characterized as high on scholarship and student selectivity, and low on awareness. It is no longer, however, at the bottom of the rank order on community. Among the college experience variables and factors, the ES schools rank at the top in the proportion of vocational majors and at the bottom in the proportion of majors in social sciences and humanities, and languages and arts. They also rank at the bottom in discussions with faculty members, academic memories that stand out, and satisfaction with the institution. Among the various outcomes the ES schools are at the top in measures related to science and at the bottom in measures related to human relations, humanistic and esthetic matters, political involvement, liberal viewpoints, and in the factor described as intellectual-liberal-independent. Overall, the ES schools are about as distinctive today as they were formerly, being at one end or the other of the rank orders on 22 out of 33 measures in the upperclassmen survey compared with 27 out of 36 in the alumni survey.

TEACHERS COLLEGES

Alumni class of 1950

Their environment is low on scholarship and on the proportion of academically oriented students in the student body. They rank high on the proportion of students majoring in vocational subjects and low on the proportion reporting conversations with counselors and on the humanistic-academic emphasis of the college experience. On the various outcome measures they show high rank on vocational benefits, civic activities, and religious activities, and a low rank on income, viewpoints with respect to civil rights, and the factors described as social awareness and attitudes, intellectual-cosmopolitan, and critical thinking-knowledge-independence.

Student class of 1970

In many respects the institutions we have classified as teachers colleges are more distinctive now than previously. The environment is low on scholarship, awareness, and academic selectivity of the student body. Rankings on the college experience measures are high with respect to the proportion of majors in languages and arts, and low in the proportion of majors in social sciences and humanities and physical and biological sciences. The TC schools also rank low on contacts with counselors, and on the factor of academic emphasis and satisfaction, but high in the proportion of students encountering academic and financial difficulties. On the several outcome measures, they rank high only on vocational benefits and involvement in religious activities; they fall at or near the bottom of the institutional rank orders on humanistic benefits, liberal viewpoints, civic activities, science activities, political involvement, and the factor described as intellectual-liberal-independent. Overall, they fall at the top or bottom ranks on 21 of the 33 measures in the upperclassmen survey compared with 17 of 36 measures in the alumni survey.

Table 28 summarizes these sketches by comparing the proportion of high and low ranks from the alumni and upperclassmen data for each institutional type—the higher the percentage, the greater the distinctiveness. In both surveys, the SLAs and the ESs are clearly the most distinctive; and the GUs and SCOUs are the least distinctive. Clearly too, the SUs have become more distinctive, and so have the TCs, while the SCOUs and the GLAs have become less distinctive.

In the next two tables we show the intercorrelation of rank orders of the institutional types on the various experience and outcome dimensions that were produced by the factor analyses of the alumni data, Table 29, and the upperclassmen data, Table 30. From the pattern of these intercorrelations, one can identify the major aspects of diversity that characterize the system of institutions, at least as reflected by the eight types of institutions we have studied. In these tables, the upper triangle of correlations are the relationships among the experience factors; the lower triangle of correlations are the relationships among the outcome or attainment factors; and the correlation within the marked-off rectangular section are the relationships between the experience factors and the outcome factors.

In interpreting these correlations one needs to remember that they are correlations between the rank order of institutional types. They are not relationships between a lot of individuals or between a lot of institutions. The number of cases is eight—not 80 and not 8,000. The correlation of 1.00, in Table 30, between the experience factor of faculty and peer involvement and the outcome factor labeled human relations simply means that the type of institution in which the extent of faculty and peer involvement is the greatest also ranks highest on the human

TABLE 28   Percent of measures on which each institutional type has a distinctive (high or low) rank

Type of institution	Alumni data	Upperclassmen data
Universities		
SU	36	58
GU	25	30
SCOU	33	21
Liberal arts		
SLA	83	76
GLA	42	30
DLA	39	36
Other		
ES	75	67
TC	47	64

relations outcome factor, and so on in parallel rank orders to the type
of institution having the lowest rank on faculty and peer involvement
also having the lowest rank on the human relations outcome factor.
When N = 8, a rank order correlation needs to be about .50 in order to
be regarded as significantly different from zero at the .05 probability
level. In other words, the chances are 95 out of 100 that a correlation
of .50 will be significantly different from zero, and the chances are 68
out of 100 that a correlation of .25 will be significantly different from
zero. We would certainly regard correlations of $\pm$.25 or smaller as
insignificant.

From the alumni data (Table 29) intercorrelations among the college
experience factors (the upper triangle) one can conclude that the major
dimension seems to be the richness of involvement in campus and
academic affairs, and particularly with strongly humanistic and social
science oriented institutions. The opposite, presumably, would be a
scientific or vocational orientation and minimal contacts with faculty
members, counselors, and campus life. Indeed, this dominant pattern of
institutional factors correlates positively and strongly with many logic-
ally congruent outcome measures, such as those related to personal and
social development, human relations, civic and political activity, and
generally humanistic and esthetic topics. The pattern is negatively
related to vocational outcomes and to nationalistic attitudes and religious activities. The various outcome measures correlate with each
other in a roughly similar pattern (the lower triangle)—the human relations, civic and community, humanistic and esthetic outcomes being
positively interrelated but not significantly associated with the more

TABLE 29 Intercorrelation of rank orders of institutional types on experience and outcome factors, alumni data

	Humanistic-social science-academic emphasis	Involvement with faculty and academic experience	Involvement with counselors	Orientation to campus life	Faculty-counselor discussions of personal and financial problems
Humanistic-social science emphasis					
Involvement with faculty and academic experience	78				
Involvement with counselors	81	33			
Orientation to campus life	57	67	-02		
Faculty-counselor discussions of personal and financial problems	74	90	31	62	
Vocational attainment	-60	-77	-74	-25	-31
Social awareness and attitudes	57	15	67	36	03
Personal-social development, human relations, and community involvement	69	95	22	79	88
Humanistic-esthetic benefits and activity	71	71	53	91	64
Personal-interpersonal-humanistic benefits	69	95	22	79	88
Civic and political activity	52	52	43	83	36
Intellectual-cosmopolitan	50	05	55	26	-02
Critical thinking-knowledge-independence	40	07	36	19	00
Chauvinism-piety	-38	06	-62	-43	15

intellectual-independent outcomes, nor as negatively related to chauvinism-piety as are the liberal-intellectual-independent factors. The system or pattern seems to fall primarily along three clusters: (1) humanistic-esthetic-interpersonal-civic, together with the general richness of campus involvement; (2) liberal-intellectual-independent *vs* conservative-nationalistic-religious, neither being strongly related to measures of campus involvement in most cases; and (3) vocational attainment—unrelated to other outcome measures and negatively related to the richness of campus experience.

From the upperclassmen survey intercorrelations, Table 30, we find

Vocational attainment	Social awareness and attitudes	Personal-social development, human relations, and community involvement	Humanistic-esthetic benefits and activity	Personal-interpersonal-humanistic benefits	Civic and political activity	Intellectual-cosmopolitan	Critical thinking-knowledge-independence	Chauvinism-piety
09								
-19	10							
-11	57	74						
-19	10	100	73					
-20	24	57	90	57				
-05	86	03	31	05	15			
-02	62	06	12	10	-07	93		
05	-90	00	-52	03	-55	-81	-60	

more of a blending between the sciences and the social sciences and humanities in the college experience. Nevertheless, the nature of campus involvement—with faculty and peers, and with academic emphasis and satisfaction—is most closely related to outcomes involving humanistic, expressive, political, intellectual, liberal, and human relations factors. Science outcomes are not much related to any aspect of the college experience except majoring in science. The experience of academic and financial difficulty is negatively related to nearly everything. Among the various outcome measures there are no strongly negative relationships—although science outcomes have no connection

TABLE 30   Intercorrelation of rank orders of institutional types on experience and outcome factors, upperclassmen data

	Faculty and peer involvement	*Involvement with counselors*	*Academic emphasis and satisfaction*	*Academic and financial difficulties*	*Physical and biological science majors*	*Social science and humanities majors*	*Language and arts majors*
Faculty and peer involvement							
Involvement with counselors	26						
Academic emphasis and satisfaction	86	49					
Academic and financial difficulties	-41	21	-11				
Physical and biological science majors	31	-07	53	-58			
Social science and humanities majors	76	-10	90	-80	62		
Language and arts majors	57	-04	45	17	-18	35	
Humanistic-expressive-active	93	00	86	-58	48	90	56
Political involvement	50	-14	70	-95	71	90	00
Scientific-active	-14	-11	09	-56	76	21	-56
Intellectual-liberal-independent	63	-10	81	-76	69	95	12
Human relations	100	27	86	-42	31	76	57
Scientific-theoretical	-14	-09	15	-44	88	24	-55

with humanistic-expressive and human relations outcomes. Nevertheless, the science related outcomes do have a moderately positive connection with political involvement and the intellectual-liberal-independent factor. Also, among the outcome measures, there is a closer blending of human relations benefits and intellectual-liberal-independent benefits than was true in the alumni survey correlations. It is perhaps significant to note that neither vocationalism nor religion and conservatism appear as a major factor in the pattern of institutional relationship among the upperclassmen data. In general, it seems fair to say that some of the sharp edges have been smoothed and that the patterns of diversity and distinction are not as clear cut as they were in the alumni sample intercorrelations.

We have pulled out for separate attention in Table 31 some relation-

Humanistic-expressive-active	Political involvement	Scientific-active	Intellectual-liberal-independent	Human relations	Scientific-theoretical
67					
02	48				
79	98	49			
93	50	-14	79		
00	48	93	43	-14	

ships between the academic selectivity of the student body and various outcome measures. For the alumni data the selectivity index is the proportion of "college-prone" students; and for the upperclassmen data it is the proportion of students who had B+ grades or better in high school. It has often been argued that educational outcomes are largely predictable from the quality of students who are admitted in the first place, with quality usually defined as academic ability. The rank order correlations for the eight types of institutions in our study indicate that there are many important educational benefits and outcomes that have little relationship to the academic selectivity of the student body. There is no relationship, for example, in the alumni data, with the attainment of liberal education benefits, or personal-social benefits or with subsequent activities related to civic affairs, or to the arts. There is a

TABLE 31   Rank order correlations of institutional types between academic selectivity of the student body and selected outcome measures

Academic selectivity of the study body versus:	*Upperclassmen*	*Alumni*
Benefits: liberal education		.16
Benefits: personal and social		-.16
Benefits: humanistic	.36	
Benefits: human relations	-.69	
Liberal viewpoints	.38	.59
Activities: civic	-.62	-.09
Activities: arts	.36	.24
Activities: science	.35	.50
Activities: religious	-.98	-.86

TABLE 32   System congruence: rank order correlations between parallel sets of variables

	Alumni	*Upperclassmen*
Vocational majors vs vocational benefits	.83	.94
Science and engineering majors vs science activities	.86	.46
Orientation to campus life vs personal, interpersonal, humanistic outcomes	.69	
Faculty and peer involvement vs human relations outcomes		1.00
Awareness environment vs arts activities	.62	.67
Awareness environment vs civic activities	.62	.84

significant correlation with liberal viewpoints and with science activities, and a strong inverse relationship with religious activities. In the upperclassmen data, academic selectivity is not significantly correlated with humanistic benefits, liberal viewpoints, or activities related to science and the arts. Selectivity is negatively related to human relations benefits and to religious activities. It has a significant positive relationship only to civic activities.

What is more clearly related to some of these, and other, outcomes are certain parallel characteristics of the college environment and experience. As shown in Table 32, civic and arts activities are significantly related to the environmental characteristic described as awareness. Personal, interpersonal, and human relations outcomes are significantly related to an institutional experience characterized by orientation to campus life and faculty and peer involvement. Science activities are related to having majored in engineering and the sciences; and vocational benefits are related to having majored in some vocational field. There are, then, some system congruences between environment, experience, and outcome. These and similar congruences indicate that there is a differentiated system, rather than a monolithic one; but as we shall conclude in the next chapter, the differentiation appears to be diminishing.

6. The Decline of Diversity and Distinctiveness

Throughout this report we have presented data about eight different types of institutions: data about their environment, about their programs, aspects of campus life, and other dimensions of college experience; about the benefits their alumni and students attribute to the college experience, the present activities and viewpoints of their graduates and their upperclassmen, and other measures of progress and performance. In the final chapter our main purpose is to add up the evidence as it bears on our central topic of diversity and distinctiveness among the institutions. How much diversity is there, and along what lines, in the system of higher education? How distinctive, and in what respects, are certain types of institutions? And especially, are diversity and distinctiveness increasing or decreasing, as judged by comparing the alumni class of 1950 with the student class of 1970?

In the main body of this report we described the college environment along five different dimensions based on the College and University Environment Scales and we also characterized the environment by the proportion of college-prone, or B+, students in the student body. In characterizing the college experience we noted the proportion of students who had majored in various fields, the extent to which the campus was residential rather than nonresidential, the extent of discussions with faculty members and with counselors, academic and peer associations that stand out in retrospect, and general satisfaction with being or having been at the particular institution. We also reported self-estimated ratings of progress toward the attainment of some 17 different educational benefits, activities on several measures of involvement in civic and cultural affairs, and student and alumni viewpoints and values with respect to a number of social trends and issues. Additionally, we identified major dimensions or factors along which the institutions differed in respect to the nature of the experience and the nature of the outcomes.

DIVERSITY Here, in brief summary, is what has happened to diversity:

1. College environment: *Less* diversity now on the dimension of propriety.

2. Academic selectivity of the student body: About the same.

3. Major fields: *Less* diversity in the proportion of vocational majors (range of 11 percent to 59 percent now *vs* 17 percent to 87 percent then). *Less* diversity in the proportion of majors in social science, language, humanities and arts (range of 20 percent to 66 percent now *vs* 2 percent to 62 percent then).

4. Campus residence: *Less** diversity (range of 52 percent to 90 percent now *vs* 29 percent to 80 percent then).

5. Memories-academic: No difference.

6. Memories-peers: *Less** diversity.

7. Discussions-faculty: About the same.

8. Discussions-counselors: *More* diversity on most topics.

9. Satisfaction: *More* diversity.

10. Experience factors: *Less* diversity (average range of z scores 1.78 now *vs* 2.10 then).

11. Educational benefits: *Less* diversity (average spread of 23 percent now *vs* 34 percent then, for the 17 benefit items).

12. Activity scores: In most cases the diversity is about the same, with the following exceptions—*Less* diversity on music, *Less* on science, *More* diversity on politics, *More* on international-intercultural.

13. Social trends: *More* diversity (average range of 17 percent now *vs* 9 percent then).

14. Viewpoints on social issues: About the same overall (21 percent *vs* 17 percent); but different on certain issues—*Less* diversity on free speech, *More* diversity on viewpoints about minorities.

15. Outcome factors: *More* diversity (average range of z scores 2.66 now *vs* 2.46 then).

In the above list there are 10 instances of *less* diversity and 7 instances of *more* diversity. Since two of the examples of *less* diversity were of doubtful validity, the overall results seem to indicate that examples of *less* diversity are about matched by examples of *more* diversity. Looking only at the outcome measures, items 11 through 15

*This difference is probably due to a bias in the upperclassmen sample.

above; there are four instances of *less* diversity and five instances of *more* diversity. Among the environment and experience measures, items 1 through 10, there are six examples (or four if one omits the doubtful ones) of *less* diversity and two examples of *more* diversity. On balance, we conclude that there has been some reduction of diversity in the college environment and nature of the college experience, but that the diversity in outcomes has been maintained.

DISTINCTIVENESS To what extent are the institutions within a type more homogeneous?

1. Major fields

SU *more* distinctive now. The major fields for the alumni were 58 percent in the arts and sciences and 44 percent in vocational fields. There is greater homogeneity or distinctiveness now with 80 percent in the arts and sciences.

SCOU *less* distinctive now. Formerly the bulk of their students (66 percent) were in vocational fields. Now, there are 52 percent in vocational fields with the rest in arts and sciences.

ES *less* distinctive now. Previously nearly all their students were majors in engineering and sciences (89 percent); now this has dropped to 62 percent.

TC *less* distinctive now. The proportion of majors in education was 59 percent and now is 37 percent.

2. Experience factors

SCOU *less* distinctive now. In the alumni survey, these institutions on the average extended over 30 percent of the total range of differences between all institutions. Now they spread over 45 percent of the total range.

SLA *less* distinctive now. They now spread over 48 percent of the total range compared with 37 percent formerly.

ES *more* distinctive now. Despite the greater range of majors within them, the ES schools now fall within 22 percent of the total range of differences between all institutions, compared with 35 percent previously.

3. Educational benefits

SU *more* distinctive now. The number of benefits on which the responses of SU students deviated from the national baseline by ±5 points or more was 9, compared with only 3 in the alumni survey.

GU *less* distinctive now. Deviation on only 2 items now, compared with 8 in the alumni survey.

SCOU *less* distinctive now. Deviation on 5 items now *vs* 7 items then.

SLA *less* distinctive now. Deviation on 10 items now *vs* 14 then.

GLA *less* distinctive now. Deviation on 6 items now *vs* 9 then.

DLA *less* distinctive now. Deviation on 7 items now *vs* 9 then.

ES *less* distinctive now. Deviation on 10 items now *vs* 15 then.

TC *less* distinctive now. Deviation on 6 items now *vs* 10 then.

4. Outcome factors

SU *more* distinctive now. On the average, the SUs now fall within 20 percent of the total range of institutional differences, compared with 27 percent in the alumni survey.

SLA *less* distinctive now. They now spread over 42 percent of the total range compared with 36 percent previously.

DLA *more* distinctive now. Despite the fact that they resemble GLAs now more than formerly, they are as a group more homogeneous, covering 36 percent of the total range now compared with 56 percent formerly.

ES *more* distinctive now. Again, despite the broadening of their major fields they are, as a type, somewhat more homogeneous or distinctive now (40 percent) than previously (48 percent).

TC *more* distinctive now. There is only a small difference here—39 percent *vs* 44 percent.

5. Rank orders

The index of distinctiveness here is the percent of measures on which the institutional type has a very high or very low rank—the higher the percentage the greater the distinctiveness.

SU *more* distinctive. 58 percent now *vs* 36 percent for alumni data.

SCOU *less* distinctive. 21 percent now *vs* 33 percent for alumni data.

TC *more* distinctive. 64 percent now *vs* 47 percent for alumni data.

In the above list there are 14 examples of *less* distinctiveness and 9 examples of *more* distinctiveness. The selective universities are clearly more distinctive now than they were previously. The state colleges and other universities are clearly less distinctive now than they were previously, perhaps reflecting their increasingly all-purpose character. The selective liberal arts colleges are also less distinctive now than formerly. The DLAs, ESs, and TCs are balanced by having some more distinctive aspects and some less distinctive ones. The only institutional type that has moved in the direction of greater distinctiveness is the SUs. All others have remained the same or have lost some of their former distinctiveness.

SUMMARY   From our survey of the alumni class of 1950, there appear to have been three main clusters of diversity and distinctiveness in the types of institutions we studied. These clusters were centered around science, religion, and intellectuality, and were most clearly exemplified by the colleges of engineering and science, the strongly denominational liberal arts colleges, and the highly selective liberal arts colleges. The general comprehensive universities and the state colleges were a kind of lowest common denominator in the system. They ranked at the top of the order on almost nothing and on many measures they fell at or somewhat below the middle of the eight types of institutions, with the state colleges falling somewhat lower than the more comprehensive universities. The selective universities were not as distinctive as one might have expected them to be, although in fairness it should be noted that the ones we so classified were not nearly as selective in 1950 as they are today. The general liberal arts colleges are almost a special case. They rank more or less in the middle with respect to scholarship and awareness aspects of their environment, and on the proportion of academically oriented students on the campus. On the other hand, they rank relatively high in the extent to which their students are heavily involved in the life of the campus. They live on the campus, they participate in extracurricular activities, they have discussions with faculty members and counselors, and they retain strong memories of academic life and of their relationships with peers. Moreover, they are relatively high on the attainment of outcomes related to personal and social development, liberal viewpoints, and their alumni are actively engaged in civic activities and activities related to the arts. What this seems to say, and what appears to be confirmed by some of the other relationships in our data, is that the attainment of a broad range of personal and social benefits, of liberal viewpoints on important social issues, and of subsequent involvement in the civic and artistic life of the community seems to be related to the extent to which the college experience itself provided a rich opportunity for personal and social relationships, involvement in campus activities, and in associations with the faculty. One might argue that there was a fourth major cluster of distinctiveness and relationships, namely between the fullness of one's college experience and the subsequent feeling of having been benefited with respect to personal and social development, and to one's involvement in the life of the community.

Much of the evidence from the upperclassmen confirms this same pattern, but with some erosion of clarity. The cluster we labeled intellectuality is still evident, and the selective universities have become stronger contributors to it. Science is not quite as isolated a cluster as it was in the alumni survey. And religion is not quite as exclusively the province of the strongly denominational colleges. There is still definitely a relationship between involvement in the campus experience, faculty-academic-peers, and subsequent involvement in civic and cultural affairs, and in the attainment of personal and interpersonal benefits.

About the same amount of diversity still exists in the system despite some loss of distinctiveness in certain types of institutions. The case for arguing that there has been a general decline in diversity and distinctiveness does not on the surface appear to be strongly convincing. But beneath the surface there is reason for believing that the case is more convincing.

As higher education has developed in this country, particularly over the last 20 years, the proportion of students who have a full and rich campus experience has gradually been reduced. It has been reduced by the growth of junior colleges, by the increase in the number of part-time students, by the emphasis on vocational training, and by attendance at the large state institutions where in many cases students can live at home and thereby reduce the expense of college attendance. The consequence of this trend is that fewer students attain benefits related to personal and social development, to liberal interests and attitudes, and to involvement in civic and cultural affairs.

When student enrollments were about equally divided between private and public institutions, as they were in 1950, the distinctive aspect of some of the private colleges—selective liberal arts, denominational liberal arts, and the colleges of engineering and science—contributed more to the diversity of the system. Today, the enrollment in such institutions, including the general liberal arts colleges as well, comprises a much smaller portion of the total system and therefore the national impact of their distinctiveness has been diminished. The major enrollment increases have been in the institutions that were least distinctive in the first place and are even less distinctive today—namely, the general universities and state colleges. It is, of course, possible that within these large conglomerate public institutions there are smaller enclaves, each with some distinctive character and impact; but it is also likely that such special programs or features deviate from the common denominator financially as well as educationally. The question usually asked is how many programs of this or that special quality can the institution afford rather than the equally pertinent question of how much mediocrity or sameness can the institution tolerate. It is possible too that more diversity and distinctiveness would have been revealed by a national study that considered some set of dimensions different from the ones we have used. Given our data, however, we think it should be of some concern to those who shape public policy to note that the most distinctive institutions, which means to some extent the institutions that are most effective in achieving their purposes, are also the ones that enroll the fewest students, are in the most serious financial condition today, and whose long range future is least assured. The highly selective universities are the only significant exceptions, but they too have their share of financial difficulties. Further drift toward a least common denominator—whether in public tax policies, educational conformity, or private philanthropy—may further reduce the pockets of excellence and distinction in higher education that still remain. That, we think, would be most unfortunate.

Carnegie Commission on Higher Education

Sponsored Research Studies

*The following publications are available from McGraw-Hill Book
Company, Box 402, Hightstown, New Jersey, 08520.*

THE ACADEMIC SYSTEM
IN AMERICAN SOCIETY
Alain Touraine

HIGHER EDUCATION
AND THE LABOR MARKET
Margaret S. Gordon (ed.)

THE ACADEMIC MELTING POT
Stephen Steinberg

LEADERSHIP AND AMBIGUITY:
THE AMERICAN COLLEGE PRESIDENT
Michael D. Cohen and James G. March

CONTENT AND CONTEXT:
ESSAYS ON COLLEGE EDUCATION
Carl Kaysen (ed.)

EDUCATION FOR THE PROFESSIONS
OF MEDICINE, LAW, THEOLOGY, AND
SOCIAL WELFARE
*Everett C. Hughes, Barrie Thorne,
Agostino M. DeBaggis, Arnold Gurin, and
David Williams*

THE FUTURE OF HIGHER EDUCATION:
SOME SPECULATIONS AND SUGGESTIONS
Alexander M. Mood

THE RISE OF THE ARTS
ON THE AMERICAN CAMPUS
Jack Morrison

THE UNIVERSITY AND THE CITY:
EIGHT CASES OF INVOLVEMENT
*George Nash, Dan Waldorf,
and Robert E. Price*

THE BEGINNING OF THE FUTURE: A
HISTORICAL APPROACH TO GRADUATE
EDUCATION IN THE ARTS AND SCIENCES
Richard J. Storr

ACADEMIC TRANSFORMATION:
SEVENTEEN INSTITUTIONS UNDER
PRESSURE
David Riesman and Verne A. Stadtman (eds.)

THE UNIVERSITY AS AN ORGANIZATION
James A. Perkins (ed.)

WHERE COLLEGES ARE AND
WHO ATTENDS:
EFFECTS OF ACCESSIBILITY ON
COLLEGE ATTENDANCE
*C. Arnold Anderson, Mary Jean
Bowman and Vincent Tinto*

THE EMERGING TECHNOLOGY:
INSTRUCTIONAL USE OF THE
COMPUTER IN HIGHER
EDUCATION
Roger E. Levien

NEW DIRECTIONS IN LEGAL
EDUCATION
Herbert L. Packer and Thomas Ehrlich

A STATISTICAL PORTRAIT OF
HIGHER EDUCATION
Seymour E. Harris

EDUCATION AND EVANGELISM:
A PROFILE OF PROTESTANT COLLEGES
C. Robert Pace

THE HOME OF SCIENCE:
THE ROLE OF THE UNIVERSITY
Dael Wolfle

PROFESSIONAL EDUCATION:
SOME NEW DIRECTIONS
Edgar H. Schein

THE NONPROFIT RESEARCH
INSTITUTE: ITS ORIGIN, OPERATION,
PROBLEMS, AND PROSPECTS
Harold Orlans

THE INVISIBLE COLLEGES:
A PROFILE OF SMALL, PRIVATE
COLLEGES WITH LIMITED RESOURCES
Alexander W. Astin and Calvin B. T. Lee

AMERICAN HIGHER EDUCATION:
DIRECTIONS OLD AND NEW
Joseph Ben-David

COLLEGES OF THE FORGOTTEN
AMERICANS:
A PROFILE OF STATE COLLEGES
AND REGIONAL UNIVERSITIES
E. Alden Dunham

FROM BACKWATER TO MAINSTREAM:
A PROFILE OF CATHOLIC HIGHER
EDUCATION
Andrew M. Greeley

THE ECONOMICS OF THE MAJOR
PRIVATE UNIVERSITIES
William G. Bowen
(Out of print, but available from University
Microfilms.)

THE FINANCE OF HIGHER EDUCATION
Howard R. Bowen
(Out of print, but available from University
Microfilms.)

ALTERNATIVE METHODS OF FEDERAL
FUNDING FOR HIGHER EDUCATION
Ron Wolk
(Out of print, but available from University
Microfilms.)

INVENTORY OF CURRENT RESEARCH
ON HIGHER EDUCATION 1968
Dale M. Heckman and Warren Bryan Martin
(Out of print, but available from University
Microfilms.)

*The following technical reports are available from the Carnegie Commission on
Higher Education, 2150 Shattuck Avenue, Berkeley, California 94704.*

THE DEMISE OF DIVERSITY?
A COMPARATIVE PROFILE OF
EIGHT TYPES OF INSTITUTIONS
C. Robert Pace

FLYING A LEARNING CENTER:
DESIGN AND COSTS OF AN
OFF-CAMPUS SPACE FOR LEARNING
Thomas J. Karwin

POLITICAL IDEOLOGIES OF
GRADUATE STUDENTS:
CRYSTALLIZATION, CONSISTENCY,
AND CONTEXTUAL EFFECTS
Margaret A. Fay and Jeff A. Weintraub

A CLASSIFICATION OF INSTITUTIONS
OF HIGHER EDUCATION

PROFESSORS, UNIONS, AND
AMERICAN HIGHER EDUCATION
*Everett Carll Ladd, Jr. and
Seymour Martin Lipset*

SOURCES OF FUNDS TO COLLEGES
AND UNIVERSITIES
June O'Neill

THE NEW DEPRESSION IN HIGHER
EDUCATION–TWO YEARS LATER
Earl F. Cheit

ESTIMATING THE RETURNS TO
EDUCATION:
A DISAGGREGATED APPROACH
Richard S. Eckaus
(Out of print, but available from University
Microfilms.)

AN INVENTORY OF ACADEMIC
INNOVATION AND REFORM
Ann Heiss
(Out of print, but available from University
Microfilms.)

TRENDS AND PROJECTIONS OF PHYSI-
CIANS IN THE UNITED STATES 1967-2002
Mark S. Blumberg

PAPERS ON EFFICIENCY IN THE
MANAGEMENT OF HIGHER EDUCATION
*Alexander M. Mood, Colin Bell,
Lawrence Bogard, Helen Brownlee,
and Joseph McCloskey*
(Out of print, but available from University
Microfilms.)

AMERICAN COLLEGE AND
UNIVERSITY ENROLLMENT
TRENDS IN 1971
Richard E. Peterson
(Out of print, but available from University Microfilms.)

MAY 1970:
THE CAMPUS AFTERMATH OF
CAMBODIA AND KENT STATE
Richard E. Peterson and John A. Bilorusky

RESOURCE USE IN HIGHER EDUCATION:
TRENDS IN OUTPUT AND INPUTS,
1930-1967
June O'Neill
(Out of print, but available from University Microfilms.)

MENTAL ABILITY AND HIGHER
EDUCATIONAL ATTAINMENT IN THE
20TH CENTURY
Paul Taubman and Terence Wales
(Out of print, but available from University Microfilms.)

The following reprints are available from the Carnegie Commission on Higher Education, 2150 Shattuck Avenue, Berkeley, California 94704. (First copies of reprints are sent free on request. Enclose 20 cents each for additional copies to defray costs of postage and handling.)

PROBLEMS IN THE TRANSITION FROM ELITE TO MASS HIGHER EDUCATION, *by Martin Trow. A paper prepared for a conference on mass higher education sponsored by the Organisation for Economic Co-operation and Development, June 1973.*

MEASURING FACULTY UNIONISM: QUANTITY AND QUALITY, *by Bill Aussieker and J. W. Garbarino, reprinted from* INDUSTRIAL RELATIONS, *vol. 12, no. 2, May 1973.*

COMING OF MIDDLE AGE IN HIGHER EDUCATION, *by Earl F. Cheit, address delivered to American Association of State Colleges and Universities and National Association of State Universities and Land-Grant Colleges, Washington, D.C., November 13, 1972.*

THE DISTRIBUTION OF ACADEMIC TENURE IN AMERICAN HIGHER EDUCATION, *by Martin Trow, reprinted from Bardwell Smith (ed.),* THE TENURE DEBATE, *Jossey-Bass, San Francisco, 1972.*

THE NATURE AND ORIGINS OF THE CARNEGIE COMMISSION ON HIGHER EDUCATION, *by Alan Pifer, based on a speech delivered to the Pennsylvania Association of Colleges and Universities, Oct. 16, 1972, reprinted by permission of The Carnegie Foundation for the Advancement of Teaching.*

MORE FOR LESS: HIGHER EDUCATION'S NEW PRIORITY, *by Virginia B. Smith, reprinted from* UNIVERSAL HIGHER EDUCATION: COSTS AND BENEFITS, *American Council on Education, Washington, D.C., 1971.*

ACADEMIA AND POLITICS IN AMERICA, *by Seymour M. Lipset, reprinted from Thomas J. Nossiter (ed.),* IMAGINATION AND PRECISION IN THE SOCIAL SCIENCES, *pp. 211-289, Faber and Faber, London, 1972.*

POLITICS OF ACADEMIC NATURAL SCIENTISTS AND ENGINEERS, *by Everett C. Ladd, Jr., and Seymour M. Lipset, reprinted from Science, vol. 176, no. 4039, pp. 1091-1100, June 9, 1972.*

THE INTELLECTUAL AS CRITIC AND REBEL: WITH SPECIAL REFERENCE TO THE UNITED STATES AND THE SOVIET UNION, *by Seymour M. Lipset and Richard B. Dobson, reprinted from* DAEDALUS, *vol. 101, no. 3, pp. 137-198, Summer 1972.*

POLITICS OF AMERICAN SOCIOLOGISTS, *by Seymour M. Lipset and Everett C. Ladd, Jr., reprinted from* AMERICAN JOURNAL OF SOCIOLOGY, *vol. 78, no. 1, pp. 67-104, July 1972.*

FACULTY UNIONISM: FROM THEORY TO PRACTICE, *by Joseph W. Garbarino, reprinted from* INDUSTRIAL RELATIONS, *vol. 11, no. 1, pp. 1-17, February 1972.*

INTERNATIONAL PROGRAMS OF U.S. COLLEGES AND UNIVERSITIES: PRIORITIES FOR THE SEVENTIES, *by James A. Perkins, Occasional Paper No. 1, July 1971, reprinted by permission of the International Council for Educational Development.*

ACCELERATED PROGRAMS OF MEDICAL EDUCATION, *by Mark S. Blumberg, reprinted from* JOURNAL OF MEDICAL EDUCATION, *vol. 46, no. 8, August 1971.* *

SCIENTIFIC MANPOWER FOR 1970-1985, *by Allan M. Cartter, reprinted from* SCIENCE, *vol. 172, no. 3979, pp. 132-140, April 9, 1971.*

A NEW METHOD OF MEASURING STATES' HIGHER EDUCATION BURDEN, *by Neil Timm, reprinted from* THE JOURNAL OF HIGHER EDUCATION, *vol. 42, no. 1, pp. 27-33, January 1971.* *

REGENT WATCHING, *by Earl F. Cheit, reprinted from* AGB REPORTS, *vol. 13, no. 6, pp. 4-13, March 1971.* *

COLLEGE GENERATIONS–FROM THE 1930's TO THE 1960's, *by Seymour M. Lipset and Everett C. Ladd, Jr., reprinted from* THE PUBLIC INTEREST, *no. 24, Summer 1971.*

AMERICAN SOCIAL SCIENTISTS AND THE GROWTH OF CAMPUS POLITICAL ACTIVISM IN THE 1960s, *by Everett C. Ladd, Jr., and Seymour M. Lipset, reprinted from* SOCIAL SCIENCES INFORMATION, *vol. 10, no. 2, April 1971.*

THE POLITICS OF AMERICAN POLITICAL SCIENTISTS, *by Everett C. Ladd, Jr., and Seymour M. Lipset, reprinted from PS, vol. 4, no. 2, Spring 1971.* *

THE DIVIDED PROFESSORIATE, *by Seymour M. Lipset and Everett C. Ladd, Jr., reprinted from CHANGE, vol. 3, no. 3, pp. 54-60, May 1971.* *

JEWISH ACADEMICS IN THE UNITED STATES: THEIR ACHIEVEMENTS, CULTURE AND POLITICS, *by Seymour M. Lipset and Everett C. Ladd, Jr., reprinted from* AMERICAN JEWISH YEAR BOOK, *1971.*

THE UNHOLY ALLIANCE AGAINST THE CAMPUS, *by Kenneth Keniston and Michael Lerner, reprinted from* NEW YORK TIMES MAGAZINE, *November 8, 1970.*

PRECARIOUS PROFESSORS: NEW PATTERNS OF REPRESENTATION, *by Joseph W. Garbarino, reprinted from* INDUSTRIAL RELATIONS, *vol. 10, no. 1, February 1971.* *

. . . AND WHAT PROFESSORS THINK: ABOUT STUDENT PROTEST AND MANNERS, MORALS, POLITICS, AND CHAOS ON THE CAMPUS, *by Seymour Martin Lipset and Everett Carll Ladd, Jr., reprinted from* PSYCHOLOGY TODAY, *November 1970.* *

DEMAND AND SUPPLY IN U.S. HIGHER EDUCATION: A PROGRESS REPORT, *by Roy Radner and Leonard S. Miller, reprinted from* AMERICAN ECONOMIC REVIEW, *May 1970.* *

RESOURCES FOR HIGHER EDUCATION: AN ECONOMIST'S VIEW, *by Theodore W. Schultz, reprinted from* JOURNAL OF POLITICAL ECONOMY, *vol. 76, no. 3, University of Chicago, May/June 1968.* *

INDUSTRIAL RELATIONS AND UNIVERSITY RELATIONS, *by Clark Kerr, reprinted from* PROCEEDINGS OF THE 21ST ANNUAL WINTER MEETING OF THE INDUSTRIAL RELATIONS RESEARCH ASSOCIATION, *pp. 15-25.* *

NEW CHALLENGES TO THE COLLEGE AND UNIVERSITY, *by Clark Kerr, reprinted from Kermit Gordon (ed.),* AGENDA FOR THE NATION, *The Brookings Institution, Washington, D.C., 1968.* *

PRESIDENTIAL DISCONTENT, *by Clark Kerr, reprinted from David C. Nichols (ed.),* PERSPECTIVES ON CAMPUS TENSIONS: PAPERS PREPARED FOR THE SPECIAL COMMITTEE ON CAMPUS TENSIONS, *American Council on Education, Washington, D.C., September 1970.* *

STUDENT PROTEST–AN INSTITUTIONAL AND NATIONAL PROFILE, *by Harold Hodgkinson, reprinted from* THE RECORD, *vol. 71, no. 4, May 1970.* *

WHAT'S BUGGING THE STUDENTS?, *by Kenneth Keniston, reprinted from* EDUCATIONAL RECORD, *American Council on Education, Washington, D.C., Spring 1970.* *

THE POLITICS OF ACADEMIA, *by Seymour Martin Lipset, reprinted from David C. Nichols (ed.),* PERSPECTIVES ON CAMPUS TENSIONS: PAPERS PREPARED FOR THE SPECIAL COMMITTEE ON CAMPUS TENSIONS, *American Council on Education, Washington, D.C., September 1970.* *

*The Commission's stock of this reprint has been exhausted.